How to (

How to Get the Most Out of Cognitive Behaviour Therapy (CBT): A client's guide is aimed at those who are either considering consulting a cognitive behaviour therapist or who are actually consulting such a therapist. Written by one of the world's leading CBT practitioners, it will steer you through the CBT process. The guide will help you to decide whether CBT is right for you, give you advice about how to make a therapeutic agreement with a therapist, show you how to prepare for CBT sessions and how to apply what you have learned from CBT after therapy has ended.

How to Get the Most Out of Cognitive Behaviour Therapy (CBT) is a concise and practical guide that will help you to understand the CBT process and how to make the most of your therapy, no matter which CBT approach your therapist practises, so that you continue to benefit from it once therapy has ended and can learn to be your own therapist.

Windy Dryden is in full-time clinical and consultative practice and is an international authority on Cognitive Behaviour Therapy. He is Emeritus Professor of Psychotherapeutic Studies at Goldsmiths, University of London. He has worked in psychotherapy for more than 40 years and is the author and editor of over 200 books.

"World renowned psychologist, Windy Dryden, has provided clients with an outstanding guide: *How to Get the Most Out of CBT: A Client's Guide*. This practical, concise and very helpful roadmap to your experience in CBT will be an invaluable tool for the many people who can benefit from this powerful approach. This is the kind of book that will help you ask the right questions and help you understand how you can best participate in this active and engaging therapy. Excellent!"

—Robert L. Leahy, Ph.D., Director, American Institute for Cognitive Therapy, Clinical Professor of Psychology, Department of Psychiatry, Weill-Cornell University Medical College, New York Presbyterian Hospital, USA

"Dryden's book *How to Get the Most Out of CBT: A Client's Guide* fills a unique and much neglected niche. There are nowadays many quality, evidence-based book on self-help, written for the clients, but there has been little for the person who after perhaps reading one or several self-help books, decides they need, after all, to seek a professional therapist. At this point they will usually have a host of questions and worries: what kind of therapist, what kind of therapy, what can I expect, what will be expected of me. Dryden address all these concerns in an accessible and engaging writing style, covering comprehensively most if not all the points a potential client might have in mind, plus many others he or she would be advised to think about. I would personally recommend this book for the majority of people who have reached that stage of seeking therapy within the Cognitive Behaviour Therapy family of therapies."

—Peter Trower, Honorary Professor of Clinical Psychology, Founder of the Centre for REBT, University of Birmingham

"Informed by a leading expert's forty years of experience in practice, writing and teaching, this is not merely a collection of techniques, but genuinely useful guidance on how to gain greater benefit from the journey of problem solving and personal growth that is CBT."

—Rob Willson, Cognitive Behavioural Therapist

How to Get the Most Out of CBT

A client's guide

Windy Dryden

Routledge
Taylor & Francis Group

LONDON AND NEW YORK

First published 2015
by Routledge
711 Third Avenue, New York, NY 10017

and by Routledge
27 Church Road, Hove, East Sussex, BN3 2FA

Routledge is an imprint of the Taylor & Francis Group, an informa business

British Library Cataloguing in Publication Data
A catalogue record for this book is available from the British Library

Library of Congress Cataloging in Publication Data
Dryden, Windy.
  How to get the most out of CBT : a client's guide / Windy Dryden.
    pages cm
  1. Cognitive therapy—Popular works.   I. Title.
  RC489.C63D79 2015
  616.89'1425—dc23
  2014036342

ISBN: 978-1-138-80402-9 (hbk)
ISBN: 978-1-138-80403-6 (pbk)
ISBN: 978-1-315-74954-9 (ebk)

Typeset in New Century Schoolbook and Frutiger
by Apex CoVantage, LLC

Printed and bound in the United States of America by Publishers Graphics, LLC on sustainably sourced paper.

Dedication

I dedicate this book to my clients past, present and future
and to the MSc REBT/RECBT students whose education
I had the pleasure of overseeing at Goldsmiths, University
of London from 1995 to 2014 and to those who taught and
supervised these students.

Contents

Introduction

I have written this book for people who are either considering consulting a cognitive behaviour therapist or who are actually consulting such a therapist. You can either read the book in one go, seek advice from a particular chapter or section that deals with an issue with which you are currently concerned or read it first and then seek advice.

What This Book Does

I have written this book to help guide you through the cognitive behaviour therapy (CBT) process from the point at which you are trying to decide if CBT is for you to the point where you have largely gone through the process and are learning how to be your own therapist. In doing so, I have discussed a variety of points of which I think CBT clients should ideally be aware. These are, of course, personal, and other CBT therapists would no doubt choose other points. What lies behind my choice of points to discuss in this book is not only my personal knowledge and experience as a CBT therapist and a trainer of CBT therapists, but also my knowledge of more general therapeutic issues and my willingness to learn from practitioners of other approaches to therapy.

What This Book Does *Not* Do

What I have *not* done in this book is to discuss any specific CBT methods that you can use to help you deal with your problems or to take any specific CBT line. In my view, CBT is a psychotherapy tradition and not a specific psychotherapy approach. It is an umbrella term under which specific CBT approaches such as Beck's Cognitive Therapy, Acceptance and Commitment Therapy, Mindfulness-based CBT, Metacognitive Therapy and Rational Emotive Behaviour Therapy can be placed. This book aims to guide you through the process no matter which CBT approach your therapist practises.

Windy Dryden
London, Eastbourne

Decide If CBT Is for You

How is it that you have ended up either consulting or thinking of consulting a cognitive behaviour therapist? How much do you know about CBT? Have you actively sought out a CBT therapist or were you recommended to do so? These are some of the questions that come to my mind as I invite you to decide whether or not CBT is for you. Indeed, these are some of the questions that I do ask people who come to see me, either to consult me as a CBT practitioner or to seek my help to determine which approach to therapy is best suited to them. Since I don't know your answers to these questions, let me deal with the issue of how you can best decide if CBT is for you in a more general way.

Common Factors That Span Different Psychotherapeutic Approaches

In the field of psychotherapy and counselling, it is recognised that different approaches have both common factors (i.e. common to all therapeutic approaches) and specific factors (i.e. specific to the particular approach under consideration). The main common factors include:

- the development and maintenance of an effective working alliance between you and your therapist;
- the provision of a safe space in which you can discuss whatever is important to you;
- the mobilisation of hope whereby you come to see that you can effectively address your concerns; and

- experiencing your therapist as someone who is genuine with you, understands you and accepts you.

As I have said, these factors are common to all approaches to therapy and are not specific to CBT.

While I have entitled this chapter "Decide If CBT Is for You," when it comes to the presence or absence of these common factors, I suggest that your focus be more on deciding whether or not the *therapist* whom you have come to see is the right *person* for you to consult than on whether or not CBT is right for you. Thus, your therapist may be technically proficient in CBT, but if you don't feel safe talking to her[1] about what really matters to you, you are right to have doubts about your therapist. Based on the above, here are some questions to ask yourself to help you make your decision about whether or not to work with your particular therapist:

- To what extent does my therapist understand my problems from my perspective?
- To what extent does my therapist accept me the way I am?
- To what extent is my therapist genuine in the way she interacts with me?
- To what extent do I feel safe to discuss what really matters to me with my therapist?
- To what extent does my therapist inspire hope in me that I can effectively deal with my problems?
- To what extent does my therapist foster a working relationship with me focused on dealing with my problems?

While it is unrealistic for your therapist to score top marks on all these points, she should score highly enough for you to consider working with her over time. If she scores poorly on all these points, then, in all probability, she will not be able to help you much despite her proficiency in CBT. If the therapist scores highly on all but one or two points, then you should consider discussing your feelings with her on the points where she does not score highly. I will address the importance of discussing with your therapist matters to do with your therapy later in this book. For now, let me make two points. First, if you don't feel able to discuss your concerns with your therapist, then this may, in itself, indicate that your therapist is not right for you. Second, if you do decide to discuss your concerns with your therapist on these matters, the way your therapist responds is important. If she takes your concerns seriously and responds without defensiveness, then these are good signs that you can work with the therapist and that you can deal with any rifts in your relationship that may occur over the course of therapy. However, if your therapist appears to dismiss your concerns and/or responds defensively, then this does not augur well for the future and you should consider finding yourself a different therapist.

Having made this point, don't forget that therapists are human too and may have their off days. However, if a therapist responds dismissively and or defensively more than once, then I do urge you to think very carefully about continuing to work with that person.

CBT's Main Specific Factors

In making a decision concerning CBT's suitability for you, it is important for you to understand some of the therapy's main features. I made the point in the introduction that CBT is, in fact, a psychotherapy tradition and that there are a number of different approaches that come under the umbrella of the CBT tradition. Having said that, let me outline some of CBT's main specific factors.

CBT Focuses on the Way You Think and Act in the Context of Your Emotions and in the Situations in Which You Experience These Emotions

CBT stands for "cognitive behaviour therapy," and thus you would expect that the therapy would focus on cognition and behaviour.

Focus on Behaviour

Let's start with behaviour, as this is the easiest of the two terms to grasp. Your CBT therapist will focus a lot on the ways in which you behave, particularly in situations in which you experience your problem(s). However, your CBT therapist may also be interested to understand what may be termed "action tendencies." These describe situations in which you feel an urge to act in a certain way but don't actually do so. Such action tendencies are particularly valuable in helping your therapist discover your hard-to-identify emotions (such as envy and hurt). Understanding the difference between an action tendency and an overt behaviour may also help you see that you don't have to act on your action tendency, which is particularly important with problems of anger and self-discipline.

The focus on behaviour in CBT is particularly linked to an understanding of your goals and values. Thus, expect your CBT therapist to enquire about the extent to which your problem-related behaviour helps you to meet your goals and to what extent it is consistent with your personally held values. Consequently, during therapy you can expect your therapist to encourage you to act in ways that help you to achieve your goals and are consistent with your values as well as to help you to identify, reflect on and deal with obstacles to the execution of such behaviour.

A particular focus on behaviour that your therapist may well take, particularly if you have problems with anxiety, is to consider your use of safety behaviours (i.e. behaviours which you use to keep yourself safe from threat, but in ways that *may* serve to maintain your anxiety problems). CBT practice is strongly underpinned by research, and while studies in the past showed the negative effects of such safety behaviours, more recent studies have shown that they may be useful in encouraging you to face your fears. Effective CBT therapists keep abreast of the research literature and modify their practice accordingly.

Focus on Thinking

While the word "cognitive" is derived from the Latin verb *cognoscere*, meaning "to know," in CBT it is used to refer to your thinking and particularly thinking that has a bearing on how you feel and act. Thinking can occur at different levels of your mind. There is surface-level thinking, which occurs in the form of automatic thoughts (i.e. thoughts that pass through your mind and are easily identifiable) and there is deeper-level thinking, which is less easily identifiable and takes the form of underlying beliefs. CBT therapists may vary in how much emphasis they place on these different levels of thought. If they deal with both levels, they may differ concerning the order in which they focus on them. What is important is that your therapist helps you to understand the role that your thinking (at whatever level) plays in your problems and elicits your agreement concerning how best to deal with them.

Another type of thinking that CBT therapists are interested in concerns where you place your attention when you are experiencing your problems. This is known as your attentional focus and is a useful area for you to explore with your therapist, whatever problems you have, for what you pay attention to tends to be closely related to your behaviour and emotions.

With respect to thinking, a recent development in CBT research and practice has been on ruminations, thoughts that go round and round in your head which you just can't seem to stop. It has been known for many years that such thinking is a key component of worry or generalised anxiety disorder (GAD), but more recently its important role in the perpetuation of depression and unhealthy anger, to take but two examples, has come to be realised.

You should be aware that CBT therapists from different approaches tend to vary concerning how they address your thinking. For example, practitioners of a CBT approach known as *rational emotive behaviour therapy* (REBT), pioneered by Dr. Albert Ellis, will help you early on in therapy to identify and challenge one or more of four deeper-level unhealthy beliefs (known as irrational beliefs) using arguments designed to encourage you to consider how consistent with reality these beliefs are, how logical they are and how useful they are. These therapists will also help you to construct healthy (or rational) alternatives to these beliefs which are more consistent with reality, more logical and more useful to you.

Other CBT therapists will focus initially on your more accessible surface-level thinking and help you to examine such thinking for its practical utility and to construct more helpful alternative ways of thinking. Later on these therapists, who have been trained in *cognitive therapy*, pioneered by Dr. Aaron T. Beck, will help you to identify and again examine for their practical utility a deeper set of underlying beliefs known as schemas and to construct more useful schemas. Unlike their REBT colleagues, cognitive therapists consider that the form of such schemas can vary greatly from individual to individual rather than be grouped into one or more of REBT's quartet of unhealthy (irrational) and healthy (rational) beliefs. Also, cognitive therapists are primarily concerned with the practical utility of thinking, and while they are also concerned with how consistent with reality such thinking is, they are less concerned with the logical status of such thinking.

While I have touched on some differences between REBT therapists and cognitive therapists, both are concerned to help you to focus on thinking that underpins your emotional problems with a view to help you to stand back and respond to it in some way. Other CBT therapists believe that encouraging you to respond to such thinking only results in you getting increasingly caught up in such thinking and may unwittingly help you to ruminate. For these therapists, who practise a form of CBT known as *acceptance and commitment therapy* (ACT), problem-related thinking is best dealt with by your accepting its existence without engaging with such thoughts (e.g. by challenging them) and by committing yourself to value-based behaviour despite the presence of these thoughts in your mind. These therapists do not speak of thoughts being distorted or realistic or beliefs being irrational or rational because they consider thoughts to be very much influenced by the context in which you find yourself rather than by the realistic or rational status of the thoughts.

From a therapeutic point of view rather than a scientific perspective, what really matters is whether the explanation provided to you by your CBT therapist concerning the role your thinking plays in your problems and what to do about it makes sense to you and whether you are prepared to proceed with a therapy that is based on these ideas. That is why it is so important in CBT for the therapist to be transparent in explaining her position on these issues to you.

CBT Focuses on How You Unwittingly Maintain Your Problems Rather Than on How They Originally Began. Consequently, CBT Focuses on What You Can Do Now to Address Your Problems

It is often thought that CBT therapists are not interested in your past. This is not correct, and in CBT you may talk about whatever it is you are bothered about, be it your past, your present or your future. Having said this, CBT therapists tend not to believe that helping you to understand the past roots of your present problems will be curative in the long term without you doing something about these problems in the present. CBT therapists generally hold to the view that relevant past experiences may have contributed to your current problems but do not account fully for these problems. CBT therapists explain this by pointing out that if 100 people all experienced exactly the same past experiences as you, not all of them would have developed the same problems as you. Some may have developed other problems and others would not have developed problems at all. Rather, it is the views you took from these experiences and still hold currently that largely account for your problems together with the behaviour that stems from these views.

For example, take the problem of jealousy. If you have such a problem, it may well be the case that you felt jealous of your sibling as a child. However, this insight will not help you if you continue to act in jealous ways in the present (e.g. by preventing your partner from doing things, checking on his or her whereabouts). Such behaviour will reinforce and strengthen the beliefs that underpin your jealous feelings and will nullify any effect that insight into the possible roots of your problem might have. As a result, unless your CBT therapist helps you to deal with the ways in which you currently, but unwittingly, maintain your problem, then it is unlikely that you will gain much long-term benefit from therapy.

CBT Focuses on Helping You to Put Into Practice Between Sessions What You Learn in Sessions

When you consult a CBT therapist, it is unlikely that you will derive any benefit unless you learn something in the therapy sessions. However, such learning is likely to be academic and thus of limited value to you unless you put it into practice between therapy sessions. Consequently, in CBT, expect your therapist to negotiate with you on ways of implementing your session-derived insights into relevant situations in your everyday life. The extent to which you do so will determine how much you get from CBT. Thus, I am often asked whether CBT is helpful. What is my answer? Yes, if you use it; no, if you don't! I will discuss the issue of applying what you learn in Chapter 6.

CBT Focuses on Helping You to Become Your Own CBT Therapist

While all approaches to counselling and psychotherapy have as an aim you learning how to help yourself in the future after therapy has ended, CBT therapists, more than other practitioners, implement this aim in specific ways. They do this by teaching their clients CBT self-help skills throughout the therapy process. Thus, your therapist may well use a CBT-related framework to teach you how to assess your own problematic thinking, feeling and behaviour in problem-related episodes and how to respond productively to these situations. You will then be encouraged to use this framework for yourself between sessions and helped to refine your developing skills in subsequent sessions by your therapist when you report back on how you implemented your skills. Given this emphasis on helping you to become your own CBT therapist, it is likely that your therapist will give you increasing responsibility to help yourself as therapy progresses. She will do this by gradually fading her own active contribution to the process, becoming more of a consultant and giving you feedback on your developing self-helping skills than by actively taking the lead as she did at the beginning of therapy.

Because CBT emphasises teaching clients self-help skills, there are a number of CBT-oriented workbooks available that can be used as an adjunct to therapy. Your therapist may suggest incorporating such a workbook into your therapy. While some clients value using such workbooks, others find them too formulaic and would prefer not to use them.

Flexible CBT therapists will be mindful of the fact that while CBT does emphasise the teaching of self-help skills as an integral part of the therapy, some clients do not want to learn these skills in such a deliberate manner. These flexible therapists adjust CBT accordingly. I will discuss the issue of becoming your own CBT therapist more fully in Chapter 8.

In this chapter, I have set out to give you a flavour of some of CBT's distinctive features while acknowledging that different CBT approaches emphasise some and de-emphasise others. I have also stressed that as CBT values explicitness, it is very likely that your therapist will make clear to you how she will use CBT to understand and deal with your problems. Thus, it should be easier for you to judge whether or not CBT is for you than it would be if you were consulting a therapist who practises a non-CBT approach. If you are still in doubt, most CBT therapists will suggest a brief "trial period" of therapy where you can experience CBT for yourself as a way of judging whether or not you wish to make a firm commitment to becoming a CBT client.

If you have decided that CBT is for you and you have found a properly trained therapist[2] to work with, you will need to make a number of practical agreements with her to ensure that therapy gets off on the right foot. This will be the subject of the next chapter.

Notes

1. In this book, when I refer to the therapist, I will refer to the person as "she." This was determined by the toss of a coin.
2. I suggest that you conduct an Internet search to locate the appropriate professional bodies in the country where you are that accredit CBT therapists in order to find a properly trained CBT practitioner if you have not already been referred to one.

2

Make Practical Agreements
With Your Therapist

Therapy, of whatever type, works better if the two involved parties, namely you and your therapist, agree on a number of important points. These points can be placed in one of two realms: the practical realm of cognitive behaviour therapy and the therapeutic realm of CBT.

The practical realm of CBT involves such matters as your therapist's fee, if one is charged, and how it is to be paid; how frequently the two of you will meet; how many sessions you will have; and what the cancellation policy of your therapist is. If your therapist works in a clinic, then there may well be additional practical issues to be discussed and agreed. I will deal with such practical agreements in this chapter.

The therapeutic realm of CBT involves such matters as how you and your therapist see your problems and what your respective goals are in regard to these problems. It also involves understanding what steps you are both going to take to address your problems and help you achieve your goals and the commitment you are prepared to make with respect to carrying out these steps. I will deal with such therapeutic agreements in the next chapter.

While the distinction between the practical and therapeutic realm of CBT is somewhat arbitrary—after all, how you and your therapist negotiate on the practical issues may either be therapeutic or non-therapeutic—it is a useful way of separating out issues concerning why you have come for therapy and what you want to achieve (i.e. the therapeutic realm) and issues that are designed to grease the wheels for both of you (i.e. the practical realm) as you both strive to achieve your goals. So here are some of the practical agreements you will need to make with your CBT therapist.

The Length of Therapy Sessions

One of the practical aspects of your therapy that your therapist should make clear at the outset is the length of therapy sessions. Actually, when most therapists talk about therapy "sessions," they most often refer to the therapeutic hour as lasting 50 minutes rather than a full hour. The tradition of the 50-minute therapeutic hour has come about to reflect the fact that therapists need to take a short break between sessions for several reasons, most typically to write notes, clear their head, go to the toilet or make and/or take phone calls. If your therapist operates a 50-minute-hour practice, then she should make this clear to you. Otherwise, you may think that your sessions last for 60 minutes and may consider that you have been short-changed if your therapist stops sessions after 50 minutes without explanation. If your therapist does not make this clear, then, by all means, ask her. Sometimes therapy sessions may be shorter or longer, and if any changes are made to an established and agreed arrangement with respect to the length of therapy sessions, then this needs to be fully discussed, understood by you and your therapist and agreed to by both of you. Any changes to an established session length may result in pro rata changes to any fees that are being charged (see the next section).

The Fee

If you are seeing your CBT therapist in a National Health Service (NHS) clinic or facility or in an organisation that does not levy a fee, then what I have to say does not concern you, although if this is the case it is very likely that the number of sessions you can agree to have with your therapist will be limited (see the section, The Total Number of CBT Sessions, later in the chapter). However, if it is the case that your therapist levies a fee, then it is very important that you understand what this fee is. I have known clients who have not enquired about the therapist's fee and have had quite a shock when they received the latter's invoice because the therapist, in these cases, had not told the clients what her fees were. So please do ask your therapist what her fee is if she does not venture this information herself. I suggest that you do this on initial enquiry to save time. If your therapist's fees are out of your financial reach, it is useful to enquire about whether she has a sliding scale, but if not or if the reduced fee is still out of your range, then it is useful to ask the therapist if she has a colleague whose fees are within your range. Be prepared, therefore, to tell the referring therapist how much you are prepared to pay.

You may well be thinking that how much you can afford per therapy session will be based on how many sessions you need, but please bear in mind that therapists cannot tell their prospective clients how many sessions they may need until they have carried out a thorough assessment.

When you and your therapist have agreed to a fee, it is useful to discover if the fee (or part of it) will be levied if you contact and discuss matters with the therapist between sessions or if the fee will be charged for other matters. For example, I once saw a client for individual CBT who at the same time was having couples therapy with a different therapist. The client had to be hospitalised, but requested a couples therapy session with her couples therapist while she was in hospital. The couples therapist came to the hospital and duly conducted the session. To my client's surprise and consternation, the therapist billed the couple for three hours as opposed to the usual one hour charge for the session. When questioned, the therapist told the couple that he was billing for the one hour session and the two hours that he gave up to travel to and from the hospital to carry out the session. The point that I wish to make here does not concern the rights and wrongs of charging for two hours travel time, but concerns the fact that the therapist did not make clear that he was going to do this in advance of agreeing to carry out the hospital-based therapy session. Also, the client couple could have asked if there was going to be an additional charge, as the therapist would have to make the journey out of his professional time. This failure to make an agreement about the additional charge, which I argue is in the practical realm of therapy, had quite an adverse effect on the therapeutic realm and it took quite a while for the therapist to regain the couple's trust in him.

The Cancellation Policy

When you contract with your CBT therapist and if she does levy a fee, then it is important that you understand what her cancellation policy is. Once you understand this, you may wish to suggest amendments based on your unique circumstances. This should lead to a discussion and hopefully to a mutually agreed policy. Possible ambiguities of the terms of the policy should be highlighted by one or both parties and clarified. For example, I have a 48-hour cancellation policy, which, as I point out to prospective clients, is different from one specifying two days. Thus, if a client and I have scheduled for, say, 11 am on Wednesday and he wishes to cancel it without paying my fee, then he needs to inform me of that by 11 am on the Monday before. If he cancels his appointment at 12 noon on Monday, he will be charged, since he has not given me the full 48 hours notice.

Some therapists will not charge a fee if you cancel your session without giving full notice if you become ill or a member of your family becomes ill, for example, while others will still levy their fee under these circumstances. It is important that your therapist is clear with you about the exceptions she is prepared to make concerning fee payment when you have not given full notice, and if she does not do this, then in my view you should ask her.

Some therapists apply their cancellation policy to themselves, while others don't. For example, if I have to cancel a client's session and I have not given him 48 hours notice, then his next scheduled session is given free of charge. Again, the therapist should ideally make this explicit to you as her client.

The Total Number of CBT Sessions

If you are thinking about consulting a CBT therapist, it is likely that you are wondering how many sessions you are likely to need. However, while this is a reasonable question to ask your therapist, it is important for you to realise that the number of sessions you will need cannot be validly determined by your therapist when you first contact her and give her very rudimentary information about yourself and your problems. As I have stated previously, it can only be answered after your therapist has met with you and carried out a full assessment of your problems and what you want to achieve from therapy. Having said that, here is what I say to prospective clients:

The length of therapy depends on how many problems you have, what you want to achieve with respect to these problems, how chronic your problems are and how hard you work in therapy. So if you have a few problems that are acute in nature, are prepared to work hard to address these problems in between therapy sessions and to work towards achievable, specific goals, then therapy is likely to be short term in nature. However, if you have a large number of problems that are chronic in nature, you think that change will occur in therapy sessions rather than by what you do between sessions and your goals are vague, then therapy is likely to be longer term.

The Frequency of CBT Sessions

Normally, you will see your CBT therapist once a week until you make progress, and then sessions are likely to be spaced out more. This is because a major goal of CBT is for you to become your own therapist, as I mentioned in Chapter 1 and as I will discuss more fully in Chapter 8. As you learn the skills of CBT, you will be encouraged to take increasing responsibility for applying them in your life, and the increasing spacing out of therapy sessions encourages you to do that.

There may be times when you may see your therapist more than once a week. This may reflect the complexity of your problems or that you are going through a crisis; both of these situations indicate that you need more therapeutic input than weekly sessions. However, even under these conditions, you will be encouraged to take responsibility for dealing with these issues as far as you are able and to reduce the frequency of sessions when you are ready to do so. This readiness will be assessed by you and your therapist together.

Confidentiality

You may think that the contact between you and your CBT therapist is completely confidential, but in reality, this is unlikely to be the case. Here is a list of situations where your therapist may reveal information about you or take action without your permission:

- when mandated to do so by the courts
- to protect your well-being when you are not able or willing to do so
- to protect the well-being of others when you pose a threat to them without yourself taking steps to protect them
- if you steadfastly refuse to pay your therapist's fees so that she has to take legal action to be paid

Your therapist may have additional exceptions to complete confidentiality, and if so, she should inform you about these. This latter point is the main one that I wish to stress. One of the ethical principles that counselling and psychotherapy is based on is known as *informed consent*. From your perspective as a client, this means that you need to be clearly informed about something before you can properly consent to it. Because one of the features of CBT is its explicitness, its practitioners should, ideally, make explicit all the exceptions to complete confidentiality. However, should this not happen, take responsibility and ask your therapist directly.

The Form of the Contract

So far, in this chapter, I have focused on the practical agreements that you need to make with your therapist if you are to get the most out of CBT. While the important point is that these agreements should be made, you and your therapist need to determine together the form that they will take. Thus, such agreements may be made informally or formally.

An informally made agreement tends to be verbal and as such it is open to misinterpretation and misunderstanding. Thus, earlier I mentioned that I have a 48-hour cancellation policy. If I explain what this means verbally, the client may not understand what I have said or forget the nature of the policy. This may lead to problems later when the client fails to give the stated notice and questions why he has to pay for the cancelled session.

A formally made agreement tends to be written and may even be signed by both parties. While such an agreement is not open to misinterpretation or misunderstanding, it may well put off some clients who complain that it is too businesslike and indicates that the therapist does not trust the client. In Appendix 1, you will find an example of a formal agreement.

My point here is to state the importance of you and your therapist agreeing to the form of the contract that you have decided to make in light of the fact that both forms have advantages and disadvantages.

Having dealt with the practical agreements that you will need to make with your CBT therapist, I now, in the next chapter, consider the therapeutic agreements you will need to make with her.

3

Make Therapeutic Agreements With Your Therapist

In the previous chapter, I discussed a number of practical agreements that it is important for you to make with your CBT therapist if your working relationship with her is going to get off on the right foot and stay that way. However, most of these practical agreements are common to most, if not all, approaches to therapy and are certainly not unique to CBT. In this chapter, I am going to focus on the therapeutic agreements you need to make with your CBT therapist that do pertain to CBT and concern why you have come for therapy: to address your emotional problems and get on with the business of living. While clients who are seeing non-CBT therapists will make similar agreements, I will concentrate here on agreements that typify CBT.

As I have already mentioned, one of the features of CBT that characterise this therapeutic tradition is its emphasis on explicitness. This means that you can expect that your CBT practitioner will spell out what she means about a number of important issues, as we shall see. If you think that your CBT therapist is not being clear about something, then ask her. She should tell you. If not, she should tell you why she is not prepared to tell you. The distinct advantage of therapist explicitness is that it enables you to understand where your therapist is coming from and to agree or disagree with the explicitly expressed points she has made. In this chapter, I will discuss the nature of the therapeutic agreements that you need to make with your therapist that ideally are very much facilitated by her explicit style of communication. Later on in this chapter, I will discuss the importance of speaking up if there is anything you don't understand about what your therapist is saying, if you disagree with anything that she says or if you find anything that she says or does unhelpful.

The Nature of Therapeutic Agreements

In this section I will discuss six different types of therapeutic agreements you need to make with your therapist. While your agreement on some points may be more explicit than on others, for CBT to be fully effective you need to have clear agreement on all six points.

Agreements About Your Problem(s)

You have probably come to CBT because you have one or more emotional or behavioural problems for which you are seeking help. It is important that your therapist listens carefully to these problems, communicates that she understands how you see these problems from your frame of reference and acknowledges that you want to address them. Later, she will, in all probability, offer you a CBT-based understanding of these problems, but at the outset, it is important that you agree on which problems you wish to address. Some therapists will introduce you to the idea of a problem list on which you put, in writing, what problems you want to cover in therapy. Please bear in mind that this list is not set in stone and you may add to it or subtract from it over the course of therapy.

Generally, only problems that are within your control to tackle should be on the list and those that are outside your control should not be included.

Alan was having problems with his partner and was very angry with her because she was very untidy around the house; Alan responded to this by yelling at her. When his therapist asked Alan what his problem was, he said it was his partner's untidiness. Alan's CBT therapist explained to Alan why she did not want to put this on Alan's problem list. She helped Alan see that his partner's untidy behaviour was under *her* control rather

> than *his*. Alan came to see that what was under his con-
> trol were his feelings (anger) and his behaviour (yelling).
> As Alan's feelings of anger and yelling behaviour were
> unlikely to help him effectively address his partner's
> untidiness with her, his therapist invited him to regard

his feelings and behaviour as problematic in this context and
thus to put his response to her untidiness on the problem list
rather than the untidiness itself.

Generally only emotional and/or behavioural problems
should be put on the problem list and not practical problems.
Thus, if you are experiencing financial problems in your life,
then this, on its own, is not a matter that can be directly dealt
with by CBT. Rather, you need to consult a debt counsellor or
financial adviser for such practical problems. However, you may
also have emotional problems about these practical, financial
problems and these emotional problems can be tackled with
CBT. They may, with your assent, be placed on your problem list.

Agreements About Goals

For every problem that you are seeking help for, it is useful to
have as clear an idea as you can of what you want to achieve
by addressing it with your CBT therapist.

I usually explain the importance of goals like this: Imagine
that you go to a railway terminus and say to the person selling
tickets, "I don't want to go to Brighton." This person will either
be at a loss as to what to do or will sell you a ticket for anywhere
that is not Brighton. In either case, you are likely to be unhappy
with the result. In the same way as expressing clearly where
you want to go to a train ticket seller, doing the same thing with
your CBT therapist will aid both of you to collaborate on working towards achieving your therapeutic goals.

To help you with goal setting, your CBT therapist may
use the acronym "SMART" to indicate the criteria for clearly
formulated goals. Here is what each letter stands for:

- **S** stands for "specific." The more specific you can be about
  your goals, the more you will be able to see how to achieve

them. Thus, goals such as "I want to be happy," while laudable, are very vague and as such will be difficult to achieve. On the other hand, a goal of "I want to deal with the prospect of criticism with healthy concern rather than anxiety and approach people who I think may criticise me rather than avoid them" is a clearly expressed goal and its specificity will help you achieve it.

- **M** stands for "measurable." The more you can measure your progress towards your goal, the more likely it is that you will persist in taking steps to achieve it. For example, the goal "I want to tidy my house" is difficult to measure, whereas the goal "I want to spend one hour a day tidying my house" is measurable and you can track your progress towards achieving it.
- **A** stands for "attainable." It is important to set goals that can actually be achieved by you. Thus, the goal "I want to be free from anxiety" is probably unachievable, whereas the goal "I want to respond to feeling anxious by working towards feeling healthy concern" is achievable.
- **R** stands for "realistic." You may set a goal that is attainable (e.g. "I want to exercise in the gym for an hour a day"), but it may not be realistic for you to achieve it. Thus you may live very far from a gym, and your work and family commitments may be too onerous for you to achieve this goal. While it is attainable in the sense that you have the ability to do it, it is not realistic in that you cannot find the time to do it. By contrast, "exercising for twenty minutes a day by running around the nearby park" may be both attainable and realistic.
- **T** stands for "time-bound." It is important for you to set a time frame for achieving your goal. If you do not do this, you may be tempted to keep postponing working towards achieving it. Thus, compare "I want to write my paper" with "I want to write my paper by the end of this month." While it is important to give yourself a specific time frame to achieve your goal, ensure that this frame is realistic and gives you some margin for error.

While your CBT therapist will keep the concept of SMART goals in mind when working with you, she will not try to impose it on you in a slavish manner. As I stress throughout this book, competent CBT therapists are flexible, and while they may think that encouraging you to develop SMART goals is the best way of helping you to get the most out of CBT, they also recognise that you may not find the development of such goals helpful, or your problems may not lend themselves to such an approach to goal formulation. In such cases, you and your therapist should ideally strive to formulate goals that make sense to both of you. You and your therapist may need to engage in some negotiation over this point, but a jointly agreed goal is more likely to be achieved than one that is either imposed on you or one that your therapist has serious reservations about.

Before leaving the topic of goals, I want to make one other important point. You are more likely to achieve your goals if you are prepared to commit yourself to achieving them and to accept the sacrifices that goal pursuit inevitably involves.

Two friends, John and Jack, struggle with procrastination and are falling behind in their studies as a result. Both want to begin key essays and do sustained work on those essays so that they can submit them on or before the deadline. John is committed to achieving this goal and is prepared to tolerate not attending a number of social events that he would like to attend in order to achieve this goal. In other words, he is willing to put up with the sacrifices that working towards achieving his goal would entail. Jack is also committed to achieving his goal but, unlike John, is not prepared to miss out on attending the same social events. In other words, Jack is not willing to put up with the sacrifices that pursuing his goal would entail.

It will come as little surprise to learn that John was successful at achieving his goal, while Jack was unsuccessful.

Agreements About the CBT Focus

An idea that is widespread about therapy in general is that when you go to see a therapist, you spend a lot of time talking about the past roots of your problems rather than about your problems as they exist in the present. The idea here is that if you understand how you acquired your problems in the first place, this will help you to address them in the present. However, CBT has attracted the opposing viewpoint: that when you go to see a CBT therapist, you talk about the present and the future but not about the past, and you focus on how you unwittingly maintain your problems rather than on how you originally acquired them. While there is an element of truth about this latter view, it is not quite accurate. First of all, your CBT therapist will encourage you to talk about whatever you are troubled about. So, if you are preoccupied with events in the past, then your therapist will help you to talk about them. Having said that, while CBT therapists recognise that your past experiences contribute to your present problems, they also argue that your current thoughts and beliefs about these experiences play a large role in why your problems persist.

So, while you will be allowed to discuss whatever you are preoccupied with in CBT and while due weight will be given to the influence of the past on the present, a distinctive feature of most approaches within the CBT tradition is that a clear focus will be placed on how you currently think and currently behave as a way of helping you to address your problems effectively. If you cannot agree on such a focus with your CBT therapist, then CBT may not be the right therapy of choice for you. If this turns out to be the case, your therapist will discuss with you a judicious referral to a therapist who practises an approach that better meets your ideas on the issue of what to focus on in therapy.

Agreements About the Therapist and Client Roles

I sometimes hear it said about therapy that it is a process that involves you talking and your therapist "sorting you out." This is very much at variance with what role your therapist plays and what role you are expected to play in CBT. Most

CBT therapists view the therapeutic relationship as collaborative, which means that you work together in the service of your psychological health. However, both parties bring different resources to this collaboration, and in this section I will outline what these resources are. Collectively, these resources add up to your respective roles.

Your Therapist's Role in CBT

- To bring her CBT knowledge to bear on the assessment and formulation of your problems and to communicate this clearly and explicitly
- To suggest and explain ways of tackling your problems and to make clear how these relate to the assessment/formulation and how they will help you to achieve your goals
- To engage you as an active participant in a collaborative relationship where you work together in the service of your therapeutic goals
- To identify and respond to anything that you are unclear about or have reservations about in the therapeutic process
- To identify potential and actual obstacles to goal achievement and to deal with these in a sensitive way
- To ask for feedback about the therapeutic process and discuss your suggestions for modifications to your therapy

Your Role as Client in CBT

- To speak openly about your problems, but to do so in a way and at a rate that is helpful for you
- To be active in the therapeutic process; to speak up and give your opinion about salient aspects of the therapy. You might think that as your CBT therapist is the expert in CBT, then she should know what she is doing, and thus, if you don't understand a point she is making, then that is your fault. Fortunately, this is a misguided view. It is misguided for a number of reasons

First, it assumes that your CBT therapist can do no wrong. Since your CBT therapist is human first and a therapist a distant second, she is susceptible to all the vagaries of being human. In other words, she is fallible and can make mistakes and get things wrong. Even the most skilful and experienced CBT therapist may, for example, explain something in a manner that you just don't understand.

Second, if you assume that your therapist is infallible and always explains things in an understandable way, then if you don't understand a point that she makes, it must be your fault. The consequence of this view is that you are mainly in therapy to be the passive recipient of your therapist's wisdom, and if you don't understand something, then there is no point in bringing this to her attention, since the fault, as I have already said, lies in you. Again the reality is very different. CBT is a collaborative exercise and you and your therapist are equal participants in the therapeutic process. As you are both fallible, you both can get things wrong, and the best way that human beings have of putting things right is to communicate about them. Let's see what this means in practice.

Fiona was seeing a CBT therapist about her performance anxiety. Her therapist assessed her problem and suggested a way of dealing with it which Fiona only understood in part. Her therapist assumed that Fiona understood fully his formulation and treatment suggestions and proceeded accordingly.

Fiona has two basic options here. First, she could say nothing and hope that she will understand more fully later her therapist's conceptualization of her problem and how she can best deal with it. Second, she could speak up and tell her therapist that she does not understand.

I strongly suggest that she do the latter. Here is how she might address the issue with her therapist:

Fiona: I'm not clear why you think that me doing what you call "over-preparing" my talk is a problem. Can you explain what that means, please?

Once the therapist re-explains her point, Fiona is not entirely convinced.

Fiona: Well, I kind of see what you mean, but your suggestion that I limit my preparation to an hour a day is not something I am prepared to do. I'll limit it, but not to an hour a day.

You can see from this brief vignette that Fiona is showing herself to be a full participant in the therapy process, speaking up when she does not understand something or does not agree with something. In this way she is discharging her responsibility as a client.

While CBT therapists value such therapist-client collaboration, they cannot check every point with their clients, so they rely to some extent on their clients speaking up and telling them when they don't understand something, don't agree with something or think that their therapists have got things wrong. If you don't speak up as a client, you will increase the chances that "resistance" will occur in therapy, which means that you will "resist" your therapist's efforts to help you because in some way you silently have not signed up to certain key therapeutic points. I will discuss this issue in the context of dealing with lack of progress in Chapter 7.

• To undertake to carry out agreed tasks in the service of your goals. I will discuss this further in the next section and again in Chapter 6. Also, to be open about reasons why you did not do the tasks if this was the case

If it transpires that there is not a good enough match between the therapist and client roles as outlined here that you think will be helpful to you in therapy, then it is important to discuss this discrepancy with your therapist and decide together what is the best way forward. If such an agreement about both of your roles cannot be made, then therapeutic progress will be severely compromised and you may be better off seeking help from a therapy who better approximates your views on such roles.

Agreements About Therapeutic Tasks

CBT involves you and your therapist doing various things in therapy sessions and you doing things between therapy sessions to help you achieve your therapeutic goals. For the purposes of this discussion, I will refer to these as therapeutic tasks. Note well my point that both you and your therapist are expected to carry out such tasks in CBT. What kind of agreements do you and your therapist need to make about tasks in CBT, whether you do so explicitly or implicitly? Here are some of the main agreements that you and your therapist need to make with respect to therapeutic tasks:

• That you both understand what your respective tasks are and agree to implement them in the course of therapy
• That you both understand how carrying out your respective tasks will help you to achieve your therapeutic goals as a client
• That you both understand what your skills and capabilities are as a client to carry out your therapeutic tasks and are both prepared to take the necessary steps to help you to implement these tasks if you cannot do so
• That you both agree to make modifications to your respective tasks should it become necessary to do so
• That you both understand that your therapist will teach you how to implement your tasks outside of therapy sessions, and the more you are able to do this, the more she will encourage you to take increasing responsibility to become your own therapist

Agreements About Ending

I mentioned in the previous section that one of the issues that you and your therapist need to agree on is when you will take increasing responsibility in therapy to become your own therapist. When this occurs, then you need to discuss how you are going to end the process. There are a number of approaches to end therapy in a planned way:

- to meet regularly (say weekly) and then set a date for the final session. A review session or sessions may or may not be scheduled
- to decrease the frequency between sessions before setting a date for the final session. Again, a review session or sessions may or may not be scheduled
- to decrease the frequency between sessions without setting a final date so that there are very long gaps between sessions, which effectively serve as review sessions

Here as elsewhere, the important issue is that you agree with your therapist on the best way to end the process for your own particular situation.

In the next chapter, I discuss what you can do to prepare yourself for therapy sessions so that you may derive the most benefit from them.

4

Prepare for Your CBT Sessions

You may think that now that you are in therapy, all you need to do is to turn up for your therapy sessions and talk. After all, isn't therapy supposed to be the talking cure? Well, yes and no! Obviously, you need to talk about what you are bothered about in your life, but one way to get the most out of therapy based on the principles of CBT is to come prepared for your therapy sessions.

What preparations you might make will, of course, depend on what problems you wish to discuss and the phase of therapy you are in. However, you might find the following guidelines helpful.

Develop a Problem and Goal List

Develop a Problem List

Before you attend your first therapy session, or as soon as possible after this session, I suggest that you make a list of the problems you want to address in therapy. This is known as a "problem list." Make sure that the problems on this list are those that *you* think that you have and that *you* want to address rather than problems that others think you have and want you to address in therapy. At this point, I suggest that you phrase these problems in your own words. If necessary your therapist will help you to reword your problems so that they are expressed in a form that will best help you to tackle them. This normally involves you and your therapist working to phrase your problems as clearly and specifically as possible.

As mentioned in the previous chapter, CBT works best if you address problems that are within your direct control to change.

Develop a Goal List

I also suggest that you develop a companion list of what *you* want to achieve from therapy with respect to these problems. So for every problem you have listed, see if you can set a goal. As you set your goals, bear in mind that the presence of a healthy state is easier to achieve than the reduction or absence of a negative state. Thus, the goal "I want to feel concerned about the possibility of being rejected" is easier to achieve than "I don't want to feel anxious about the possibility of being rejected."

Again, put your goals into your own words and your therapist will, if necessary, help you to express them in a form that will best help you to achieve them. Please remember one important point about therapy goals, though. You probably won't achieve them fully. As Marilyn Grey once said: "No one ever has it 'all together.' That's like trying to eat once and for all."

The same point that I made concerning targeting problems that are within your direct control to change also applies to the topic of goals. The more your goals are within your power to achieve, the more likely it is that you will achieve them.

Come With a Clear Idea of What You Want to Discuss in Each Therapy Session

You have met your therapist and had an opportunity to tell him or her why you are seeking help, and you have decided to work together. You could just turn up for subsequent therapy sessions without doing any preparation, but in my view, you would not get as much out of these sessions as you would do if you came with a clear idea of what you want to discuss. Such preparation can take a number of different forms, of which the following is a sample:

- Keep a log of events that you found upsetting in the week preceding your therapy session, perhaps putting these events in some kind of order in which you want to discuss them
- Select a problem from your problem list that you want to address (known as the "target problem") and choose a specific example of that problem to discuss with your therapist
- Take a specific example of your target problem or a specific event about which you were upset and try to make sense of it using the framework or model that your therapist outlined to you or developed with you
- Bring to the session anything that you want to revisit or did not understand from the previous session or sessions. This is an important point that I will address more fully in due course

Session Agenda

Now, your CBT therapist may well suggest that you develop an agenda for each therapy session that you attend. The purpose of this agenda is for you and your therapist to ensure that you cover what you both want to deal with in the session and for you both to use session time effectively. In addition to the above items, other items put on the agenda which you can prepare for beforehand include:

- You completing one or more inventories which provide your therapist with an objective guide to how your mood is changing as a result of therapy. To save therapy time, you may complete such inventories just before your therapy session.
- A review of any between-session activities you have agreed to do. I will discuss this more fully in Chapter 6, entitled "Apply What You Learn."

The important thing about the session agenda is that you and your therapist use it flexibly, not rigidly. So, if something really important comes up in a session that is not on the agenda, you should have the freedom to explore it rather than have it ruled "off limits" because it does not feature on the agenda.

Matters Arising

While I am not suggesting that a CBT session should be likened to a business meeting, if one is to set an agenda for therapy sessions, then it makes sense to have an item on that agenda entitled "matters arising." This means that you should bring to the session anything that emerged from the previous session or the intervening period that you wish to discuss. This might include:

- Anything you did not understand from the previous session
- Anything you disagreed with from the previous session
- Any doubts and reservations you had about the previous session or about therapy in general

I will discuss this issue more fully in Chapter 7. In the next chapter, however, I will outline a process view of CBT so you can see how your therapy is likely to unfold.

5

Understand the Process of Change

You may find it helpful to have some idea of the process of change in CBT so that you can anticipate the process that lies ahead. As such, I am going to outline a number of stages that you may go through as you make progress on the problems for which you have sought CBT. I want to make clear at the outset that I am not putting forward these stages as those that you must go through in the order that I present them. Rather, you should regard them as stages that you may go through, albeit in a different order to the ones presented in this chapter.

Stage 1: Admitting That You Have a Problem (or Problems) and Accepting Yourself for Having It (Them)

While most people who seek CBT do so because they recognise that they have a problem, this is not universally the case. Thus, you may have been sent for help or are consulting a CBT therapist because you consider that you have to, for some reason, rather than you want to do so. Indeed, you may feel ambivalent about seeking help: part of you wants to, while another part of you does not. It is important that you be honest with your CBT therapist about where you are on this issue so that she can help herself and you discover whether or not you have a problem, and if so, what might be stopping you from admitting to having it.

One of the major blocks to admitting that you have a problem is a sense of shame. Here you believe something like: "If

I admit that I have this problem, then it would mean that I am weak, inadequate and worthless." If this applies to you, then your therapist will help you to address this self-defeating idea before moving on to helping you to deal with the problem about which you feel ashamed.

You may also depreciate yourself even though you are readily able to admit to having a problem (which I refer to here as a "primary problem"). While this "meta-problem" needs addressing at some point, once you have disclosed it to your therapist, she will help you to determine whether it needs therapeutic attention before you address your primary problem or after you have done so. Basically, the more your meta-problem interferes with you focusing your attention on your primary problem, either in therapy sessions or between them, the more likely it is that you and your therapist need to address your meta-problem before your primary problem. However, here as elsewhere in the therapy process, such decisions are made jointly between you and your therapist rather than unilaterally by your therapist.

Stage 2: Understanding Your Problems: Assessment and Formulation

Some CBT therapists prefer to have an idea of all the problems for which you are seeking help and to understand the connections between them before helping you to tackle these problems one at a time. This is known as a case formulation. This formulation helps your therapist to plan therapy based on an overall understanding of your problems and the mechanisms that are at play in their inter-connections. Your therapist will not do this without your active participation, and perhaps the most important thing about a case formulation is that it is arrived at jointly between you and your therapist. This approach may be regarded as a formulation-based approach to CBT.

Other CBT therapists will prefer to begin therapy by focusing on the problem you want to start with and will wait to discover the connections among your problems later. This approach may be regarded as a problem-based approach to

CBT. In this approach, the therapist will help you and herself understand the dynamics of the problem that you have selected to tackle first. This is known as problem assessment. Again, you will be expected to take an active role in problem assessment providing relevant information and agreeing on the assessment which you arrive at jointly.

You will see that in both approaches, the therapist carries out problem assessment and a case formulation, but the order in which they do this is different.

Stage 3: Focusing on One Problem at a Time and the Importance of Being Specific

Whether your therapist adopts a formulation-based approach or a problem-based approach to CBT, when you do begin to tackle your problems it will likely to be one at a time and, as you do so, it is also likely that your therapist will ask you to identify a specific example of the problem. The reason for this specificity is that, in general, it provides you both with more valuable information than if you discuss your problems in general terms. You might wish to select a typical example of your target problem, a recent example, a vivid example or one that may occur in the near future. The important thing about the selected example is that it helps you and your therapist understand the factors that are at play in your problem. In discussing this specific example of your problem, your therapist may help you to do some or all of the following:

- Describe the situation in which the problem occurred and what you found most difficult about the situation
- Identify what emotion(s) you felt in the situation
- Identify how you acted in the situation or how you felt like acting
- Identify what you did to try to cope with the problem

In addition, your therapist will help you to set goals with respect to the problem which will help you to know what you are aiming for in similar problematic situations.

Stage 4: Examining Troublesome Cognitions and Developing Healthy Alternatives to These Thoughts/Beliefs and Associated Behaviour

In most approaches to CBT, what might be loosely called troublesome thoughts and beliefs (collectively known as cognitions) are seen to be at the core of people's emotional problems. Some approaches to CBT hold that these thoughts need to be identified and examined and healthy alternatives need to be developed and adopted if change is going to occur. Other approaches to CBT contend that it is our engagement with these troublesome thoughts that is the problem and that mindful acceptance of these thoughts and a commitment to valued action is what is needed. I will discuss the skills associated with these different approaches in Chapter 8. In the meantime, whatever approach your CBT therapist takes or even if she adopts a mixture of the two, the important point here is that you understand the role that such thoughts have on your problems and you agree with the suggested way to deal with them.

Note that CBT stands for cognitive behaviour therapy, and thus, you will also be encouraged to consider the role that your behaviour plays in your problems and will be helped to develop more constructive ways if appropriate. It is my view that when your thinking is healthy and your behaviour is constructive and when you marry the two consistently in dealing with troublesome events, then this constitutes the power of CBT.

Stage 5: Applying What You Learn

What you learn within therapy sessions[1] about the factors that account for the presence of your problems and how you unwittingly maintain them is, of course, a central plank of CBT, for without this you would continue to experience these problems, particularly if they are long-standing. However, unless you apply what you learn from these sessions to your everyday life, then it is unlikely that you will derive any lasting benefit from CBT. This is such an important topic that I have devoted an entire chapter to it (see Chapter 6).

Stage 6: Generalising Your Gains to Other Problems

Once you have made progress in dealing with your target problems, your therapist will help you to generalise what you have learned in doing so to other problems that you would like help with.

Fiona learned in therapy that her anxiety about meeting new people was based on her overpredicting the possibility of rejection and viewing any rejection as a catastrophe. To deal with her anxiety, she avoided meeting new people. Her CBT therapist helped her in three ways: to view the possibility of being rejected more realistically, to take the horror out of being rejected and to approach new people while practising these new ways of thinking. This resulted in Fiona meeting new people and in a significant decrease in her anxiety. Fiona's therapist then helped her to apply these three learnings—making realistic inferences, decatastrophising bad events and facing up to unpleasant situations—to her anxiety about public speaking and taking exams. She also helped Fiona to see that decatastrophising would also help her in her jealousy problem, although she had to learn some new skills in dealing with this latter problem as well.

Stage 7: Maintaining Your Gains

It is tempting to think that once you have made significant progress in dealing with your problems, then therapy is over. However, given the fact that we humans seem to have a talent for lapsing (defined as making slips and returning briefly to the problem) and relapsing (defined as going back to square one), if you do not deal adequately with these slips, then it is likely that you will relapse (see Chapter 8 for more information on this point). It is important, therefore, for you to recognise that you need to make a commitment to work consistently to maintain the benefits that you made in therapy. Also, the more you practise what you have learned in therapy in a deliberate fashion, the more likely it is that these learnings will eventually become second nature to you.

Stage 8: Becoming Your Own CBT Therapist

There is an old Chinese adage which states: "Give a person a fish and you feed him or her for a day. Teach a person to fish and you feed that person for a lifetime." If we adapt this to CBT we have: "If your therapist helps you to solve a problem with CBT, then she will have helped you with that problem. If she teaches you how to become your own CBT therapist, then she will have equipped you for life." Thus, if it is feasible and you are interested, then the final stage of the CBT process involves you learning to be your own CBT therapist. I will discuss this issue in Chapter 8.

At all stages of the change process you will experience obstacles to change, and these need to be identified and addressed if you are going to get the most out of CBT. I will deal with the most common obstacles to change in Chapter 7. Meanwhile, in the next chapter, I will deal with a most important topic: how you can get the most out of CBT in your everyday life by applying what you learn in therapy sessions.

Note

1. While I have written this book for those of you who are consulting a CBT therapist in a face-to-face setting, some of my points here are also applicable if you are following a CBT self-help course either by reading a book or by being taken through an online computer-based CBT programme.

6

Apply What You Learn

One of the most robust findings in the scientific literature on CBT is that people who put into practice between sessions what they learn within sessions get more out of CBT than people who don't do this inter-session practice. It follows from this that if you want to get the most out of CBT, then you need to apply what you learn from therapy in your everyday life.

In my view, you need to realise fully that much of what you can achieve from CBT is within your hands and that making a commitment to undertake regular practice of whatever skills you have learned in your therapy sessions is very important if you are going to derive the greatest benefit from CBT.

Let me give you an example of such a commitment from my own life because I think that it details a number of points that are relevant to the importance of undertaking a similar commitment in CBT.

A number of years ago I was diagnosed with a disintegrating disc in my back and later with a torn cartilage in my right knee. I was told that while these two conditions might be helped with surgery, I could manage both myself by doing a number of relevant strengthening exercises. Practising these exercises takes me about 25 minutes every day. I decided from the outset that

I would make a commitment to do such practice six days a week. I do so in the morning before I go to the gym or jog around the local park. My initial decision was underpinned by the following principles:

1. I did not want to subject myself to surgery with its attendant risks and uncertain outcome.
2. I wanted to take responsibility for my own recovery rather than handing over such responsibility to other people.
3. I determined that I would do these exercises whether I wanted to do them or not. I realised that I didn't have to be or feel motivated to do the exercises. I just needed to do them.
4. I learned to discriminate between good reasons for not doing the exercises (e.g. "I am not going to do the exercises because I am ill") and rationalisations for not doing them (e.g. "I will do the exercises tonight when I have more time to concentrate on them") and I resolved to respond to the latter and then take constructive action (i.e. by doing the exercises).
5. I created favourable environmental conditions that would help me to do the exercises rather than hinder me from doing them. Thus, I set my alarm to help me to get up on time. I make sure that the room where I do the exercises is suitably heated and that the relevant equipment is to hand.

The five principles that I outlined above are very relevant to the issue of applying what you learn in CBT sessions to your everyday life outside these sessions. Thus:

1. The more you keep in mind the purpose of applying what you learn, the more you will do so. For example, you might find it useful to keep a clearly written reminder of your goals to hand to help you see the purpose of putting into practice what you have learned in therapy.

2. The more you take responsibility for putting into practice what you learn in therapy, the more you will tend to do this practice.

3. If you resolve to put into practice what you learn in therapy, whether preferable conditions exist (e.g. having a feeling that you want to apply what you learn and having a sense of motivation for doing so) or not, then you are much more likely to do such practice than if you insist on the presence of such conditions.

4. The more you monitor your thoughts relating to the possibility of you not putting what you have learned in CBT sessions into practice in your everyday life and the more you learn to stand back and examine such thoughts, the more you will be able to discriminate between proper reasons for not taking action and rationalisations for not doing so. Once you become adept at making such discriminations you will be able to respond productively to your rationalisations and thus you will choose not to act on their content.

5. The more you structure your environment to help you take productive action, the more you will be able to do so. Structuring your environment depends, in part, on you understanding how to get the best out of yourself with respect to putting your CBT-derived learning into practice. Thus, I am more likely to write when I am in an environment where there is hustle and bustle around me (e.g. in a coffee bar) than when I am in a silent environment. Consequently, I seek out coffee bars in which to write. Think about the importance of structuring your environment when planning to put into practice what you have learned from your CBT sessions and choose an environment, if you can, that will help you to do this practice.

Homework Assignments

CBT therapists often refer to activities that clients undertake to put into practice what they have learned in therapy sessions as "homework assignments." Some people, however, do not like the term "homework" given the negative connotations that it has for them with respect to their school experiences, for example. If this is the case for you, inform your therapist and together choose a term that is more acceptable to you.

In this section, I will deal with two main issues: (i) negotiating homework assignments and (ii) reviewing homework assignments.

Negotiating Homework Assignments

With respect to negotiating homework assignments with you, you can expect your therapist to do the following:

Negotiate a Homework Assignment With You

Your therapist will not tell you what to do between therapy sessions. Rather, she will negotiate a suitable homework task with you.

Help Ensure That the Homework Assignment Is a Relevant One

Such a task should follow logically from what you have discussed in the therapy session. It may involve you reading something, identifying certain types of thoughts, examining such thoughts, imagining acting differently or actually doing so. The type of homework assignment should also be relevant to the stage reached by the two of you on the problem or issue you are working on together.

Ensure That You Understand the Nature of the Negotiated Task and Its Therapeutic Purpose

If you don't understand what you have agreed to do or why you have agreed to do it, it is important that you speak up and say so.

Work With You to Select a Homework Task That Is "Challenging, but Not Overwhelming" for You

Thus the task should not be too easy for you (and thus of very limited therapeutic power) or too difficult for you (in which case you will not do it).

*Introduce and Explain the "No Lose" Concept of
Homework Assignments to You*

Your therapist will explain that if you do the assignment, then that is good because it is likely that you have benefitted from doing so, and if you don't do the assignment, good can come out of that too, since this will help you to understand more about both the nature of your problem and the obstacle(s) to making progress. I will discuss this latter issue in Chapter 7.

*Ensure That You Have the Necessary Skills to
Carry Out the Homework Assignment and
Believe You Can Do It*

If you lack the skills to carry out a homework assignment, then no amount of determination will make up for this lack. If you do lack certain skills that are important for you to acquire before you do the assignment, then your therapist will help you to acquire them. If, on the other hand, your therapist thinks you have such skills in your repertoire and you don't, then it is important that you speak up and tell her.

*Allow Sufficient Time in the Session to Negotiate the
Homework Assignment Properly With You*

Novice CBT therapists know that they "should" negotiate homework assignments with their clients, but often lose track of time in therapy and realise, often very late, that the therapy session is ending and they have not helped their clients set homework. Consequently, they panic and often end up by unilaterally "giving" their clients homework assignments rather than taking their time to negotiate such assignments properly with their clients. If your therapist is experienced, then she will manage the session sufficiently to enable her to spend time on negotiating a suitable homework assignment with you. If not—and don't forget your therapist is human—remind her about the topic of homework if it looks as if she may have forgotten.

*Elicit a Firm Commitment From You That You Will
Carry Out the Homework Assignment*

It is one thing for you to agree to carry out a homework assignment, it is another thing to commit yourself to doing so. Thus, you can expect your CBT therapist to ask you for a firm commitment to do the task that you have both negotiated and to explore any reluctance that you have to do so.

*Help You Specify When, Where and How Often You Will
Carry Out the Homework Assignment*

The more specific you can be concerning when, where and how often you will carry out the negotiated homework assignment, the more likely it is that you will do so. Thus, you can expect your therapist to ask you to give her such specific undertakings. Otherwise, you may be tempted to delay carrying out the assignment, perhaps leaving it till the last minute. If this happens, it will mean, in all probability, that you won't get the most out of doing the agreed assignment.

*Encourage You to Make a Written Note of the Homework
Assignment and Its Relevant Details and to Refer to It
When Appropriate*

When clients do not carry out their homework assignments, one of the main reasons they give is that they forgot what the homework was and that they hadn't made a written note of the task. Thus, you can expect your therapist to ask you to make a written note of the agreed assignment and to suggest that you refer to this written note periodically so that you do not forget what it was when you come to do it.

*Elicit From You the Potential Obstacles to
Homework Completion and Help You Deal in
Advance With Any Such Obstacles*

In the next chapter, I will discuss the more general issue of why you may not be making as much progress in CBT as you may reasonably expect. One of the main reasons for lack of progress is failure to complete homework assignments. Thus, you can expect your therapist to explore with you, in advance, possible obstacles to homework completion and how these might be dealt with. If you have continued difficulty in carrying out such tasks, I suggest that you fill out the form in Appendix 2 and discuss your responses with your therapist.

Help You to Rehearse the Homework Assignment in the Session, If Practicable

If doing so is practicable and there is sufficient time, then your therapist may suggest that you rehearse your agreed homework assignment in the therapy session. The reason for this is twofold. First, it gives you experience of doing the assignment in controlled conditions so you can get a sense of what doing it in the outside world might be like. Second, it may help you and your therapist to identify and problem-solve an obstacle to carrying out the assignment not already identified.

Reviewing Homework Assignments

Unless you review your homework assignments with your therapist in the following sessions in which they were negotiated, it is unlikely that you will consider them to have the level of importance that they actually have in CBT. Again, it is worthwhile keeping in mind that one of the most robust research findings in CBT is that people who routinely carry out homework assignments get a lot more out of the process than those who do not. With this in mind, with respect to reviewing homework assignments with you, you can expect your therapist to do the following:

Check With You Whether or Not You Did the Homework Assignment

Unless your therapist checks with you concerning whether or not you did the task and what your experiences of doing so were, then she will be implicitly communicating to you that doing such tasks are not important in CBT when, in reality, they are. Such a review is usually done at the beginning of the next session so that you can usefully prepare what you are going to say about doing (or not doing) the assignment in advance of the session, as I discussed in Chapter 4.

Determine the Reasons Why You Did Not Do the Assignment as Agreed, If This Was the Case, and Address With You Any Obstacles

If you did not do the homework assignment, then you may expect your therapist to explore with you the reasons for this. You might usefully prepare for this discussion by completing the form to be found in Appendix 2 and bringing your responses to therapy. Ideally, your therapist's stance here should be to be genuinely interested in identifying any obstacles to homework completion with a view to helping you to address these obstacles rather than to reprimand you for not doing the assignment. If the latter is the case, speak up if you can and tell your therapist that her stance is not helpful to you. I will discuss the issue of you speaking up and giving your therapist feedback in greater detail in Chapter 7.

Check Whether You Made any Modification(s) to the Assignment and If So, Determine the Reasons for the Modification(s)

You may have done your homework assignment and you may have thought you had done so successfully, but you may have changed the assignment to make it easier for you to carry it out. In doing so, you may have reduced the therapeutic power of the assignment. Given this, you may expect your therapist to enquire in some detail about what you actually did to determine whether or not this was the case. If it was, your therapist will help you to discover what led you to make the modification and to deal with this factor if it helps you unwittingly to maintain your problem. It is important that your therapist both acknowledges what you achieved by doing the assignment as well as pointing out to you the problems raised by the modification you made to it.

Bernice agreed to deal with her anxiety about going shopping and losing control in supermarkets by practising her newly developed belief about the "horror" of not feeling in control and doing so on her own in a supermarket without access to support from others. She reported that she did this and that the prospect of losing control seemed more manageable. However, on closer questioning, Bernice admitted that during the task she had phoned her daughter for support and even though she did not speak to her daughter, she gained support from knowing that her daughter was there on the open phone line should she need her. The therapist acknowledged the stride forward that Bernice had made by going to the supermarket on her own, but discussed with her that she only thought that she could do so if she had direct contact with her daughter. This led to an exploration of Bernice's negative thoughts about doing the task without such support and a negotiated new assignment where she went to the assignment without her mobile phone based on the work she and her therapist did on her negative thoughts.

Review What You Learned From Doing the Assignment

Doing the assignment as agreed is important, of course, but what you learned from doing so is, in some ways, more important. So expect your therapist to ask you what you learned from doing the task. Sometimes what you learned may not be that helpful to you. Thus, you may learn from giving a public speech that nobody laughed and that nobody will laugh when you give the speech as a homework assignment. While it is good for you to learn that nobody laughed when you predicted that everybody would, it is unreasonable to jump to the conclusion that nobody will laugh in future. Here, your therapist might suggest that it would be helpful to prepare for being laughed at even though this event may be unlikely.

Deal With Homework "Failure"

You may have done the assignment and derived no benefit from it and thus you may consider the homework to have been a failure. As discussed earlier in this section, there are times when your therapist will carefully examine what you did, what happened and your thinking about the experience, and exploring homework "failure" is one of those times. Remember what I said earlier in this chapter about the "no lose" concept of homework completion. If your homework was a "failure," then that is bad, but the good thing to come out of it is understanding reasons for the failure and using what you and your therapist discovered in this process to help yourself more effectively in the future.

Capitalise on Your Success

While I have concentrated on some of the difficulties that you might experience in the area of homework assignments in CBT, I want to stress that very often clients do their tasks as agreed and gain a lot from doing so. When this happens, you can expect that your therapist will help you to capitalise on your success and encourage you to use your derived learning to further your progress on the problems that you are focusing on and perhaps to apply this learning to your other problems as well.

Applying what you learn from therapy sessions to your everyday life is the heart of CBT, in my view. However, as we have seen, CBT does not always go smoothly, and in the next chapter, I will focus on the issues that emerge when you don't make the expected progress from your therapy.

7

Understand and Deal With Lack of Progress

Sometimes in therapy people do not make the progress that they can be expected to have made and it is important that you realise that this may happen with you. If it does occur, you should ideally be prepared to join your therapist in looking for reasons for such lack of progress and in dealing with these obstacles to change accordingly. In this chapter, I will consider some of the common reasons for lack of progress and suggest ways in which you can best deal with them.[1] I will use the following structure in this chapter:

- Lack of progress due to problems in the working alliance
- Lack of progress due to client factors
- Lack of progress due to therapist factors

   I will discuss the most common obstacles to progress that occur in each of the above categories before discussing the more general issue of how you and your therapist can address such obstacles.

Understanding the Sources of Lack of Progress

Lack of Progress Due to Problems in the Working Alliance

Having a good working alliance with your therapist is what sustains therapy over the course, and thus if you are not making progress, it is important that you and your therapist investigate the possibility that there is a problem in the alliance that needs addressing.

The Therapeutic Bond Between You and Your Therapist Is Not Good

The bonding aspect of the working alliance concerns the feeling tone that exists in the relationship between you and your therapist. Thus, if you don't have good feelings for one another, this may have a negative effect on your progress. My view is that while you can still make progress in therapy if you and your therapist don't like one another, it is more difficult to do so if there is not mutual respect or if you do not have confidence in your therapist's expertise.

The Therapeutic Bond Between You and Your Therapist Is Too Good

You may think it strange that getting on too well might be a reason why you may not be making progress in CBT, but it certainly can happen. You and your therapist may enjoy each other's company so much that you may drift away from the primary objective concerning why you are seeking therapy— to address your emotional problems.

I introduced the following points in Chapter 3 when I was talking about the therapeutic agreements that you need to make with your therapist in CBT, but since disagreements on these points may explain lack of progress, I will discuss them briefly here (see also Chapter 3). Please note that while the disagreements that I discuss below may be clear and explicitly stated, they are more often implicit and therefore not stated.

You and Your Therapist Disagree on the Nature of Your Problem(s)

If you consider that you have a problem with guilt, for example, while your therapist considers that your problem is one of shame, you may end up by talking at cross purposes, and since these two emotions are underpinned by different thoughts/ beliefs and associated with different behaviours, this may result in you focusing on the wrong factors and may result in lack of progress.

You and Your Therapist Disagree About the Goals of Therapy

You and your therapist may agree on the nature of your problem, but may disagree concerning the goals of therapy with respect to this problem. Thus, you both may agree that you have a problem with extreme suppressed anger, for example, but while you think that the goal of therapy should be to help you to get your anger out of your system, your therapist may think that the goal should be to help you to express yourself with respectful annoyance. If this is the case, you will be going in one direction while your therapist will be going in another, which again may result in lack of progress.

You and Your Therapist Have Disagreements About the Focus of Therapy

While nothing is ruled out when it comes to you discussing your problems, as I pointed out in Chapter 1, the focus of CBT is largely on the present and the future, and when the past is discussed it is done so in a way that facilitates understanding of these two foci. Thus, if you want to discuss your past experiences extensively without regard to the present and the future, then you may not make progress if your therapist does not join you in a comprehensive examination of your past. CBT theory would also hypothesise that you may not make much progress even if your therapist does join you in this exploration, since while you are going over the past with her, you are still being influenced by the cognitive-behavioural factors that underpin your problems both in the present and going forward into the future.

You and Your Therapist Disagree About Your Respective Roles

As discussed in Chapter 3, CBT involves you and your therapist both adopting an active and collaborative role in therapy, and when this does not happen for any reason, you may not make as much therapeutic progress as when it does. While the most common occurrence on this issue concerns the client not assuming an active role, it may also happen that a therapist may not be active in the process or may fail to be sufficiently collaborative with the client.

You and Your Therapist Disagree About Therapeutic Tasks or Experience Other Problems About These Tasks

Therapeutic tasks are activities that you and your therapist engage in with the purpose of helping you to achieve your therapeutic goals. If you both do not agree that undertaking these tasks is helpful, then this may compromise your progress. Even if you do agree on this point, things may go wrong, as shown in the following vignette.

> Gerald was seeking help from a CBT therapist for depression and readily agreed with the cognitive-behavioural conceptualisation of his problems. His therapist taught him to use a form that was designed to help people identify and respond to troublesome thoughts that underpin depression, and Gerald could see the sense of doing this. However, Gerald had very poor spelling, about which he was ashamed, and this resulted in his not completing the forms as requested by his therapist. His sense of shame prevented him from bringing up this obstacle with his therapist.

Lack of Progress Due to Client Factors

When I say that you may be largely responsible for your lack of progress, it is not to blame you, but to help you to address such obstacles fair and square. With that in mind, let's look at some common client obstacles to change.

You Believe That Change Is Not Possible

If you think that change is not possible, you will not engage fully with the CBT process and consequently you will not get as much out of the process than if you do think that you can change.

You Opt for Short-Term "Solutions" to Your Problem(s)

We, as human beings, generally seek to make ourselves comfortable whenever we experience discomfort, and this is not a problem for us as long as there is no good reason for experiencing such discomfort. Since achieving your therapeutic goals generally involves discomfort, unless you are prepared to experience such discomfort, then your progress will be very limited. Signs that you are opting for the short-term solution of getting rid of the discomfort associated with your problem rather than being prepared to experience discomfort in the short term while facing your problem and dealing with it are many but include:

• denying that you have a problem,
• overcompensating for your problem
• and using safety-seeking behaviours to avoid experiencing your problem

Luke was anxious about meeting new people, especially in social settings. In order to deal with this problem, Luke would (i) avoid such occasions, or if he could not do so, he would (ii) pretend that he had lost his voice so he did not have to speak to people. He would also (iii) consume quite a lot of alcohol to "take the edge off" his anxiety, as he put it. In CBT, his therapist helped him to see that while these three behaviours kept his anxiety at bay in the short term, they did not help him deal with his anxiety problem in the longer term. Luke learned more adaptive ways of dealing with his anxiety and resolved to put this learning into practice rather than use the three short-term "solutions." However, Luke did not make as much progress as possible because it transpired that he managed to get one of his friends invitations to these social events and he spent time with that person rather than talking to people whom he did not know while practising the CBT skills that he learned in his therapy sessions and agreed to practise for homework.

You Have Doubts, Reservations and Objections to Aspects of Your Therapy That You Do Not Disclose

CBT is based on a particular way of making sense of your problems, of explaining how you may have unwittingly maintained these problems and what you need to do to address them effectively. In order to get the most out of CBT, you need to collaborate with your therapist in developing these problem-based and therapy-based understandings. When you don't make as much progress as expected, it may be due to one or more doubts, reservations or objections that you have with respect to these understandings that you have not expressed, the existence of which have negatively affected your participation in therapy.

Carol had a problem with chronic guilt and was easily manipulated by others, with the result that she would always put others before herself. She worked closely with her CBT therapist to develop a conceptualisation of her problems, and together they worked to devise a way of addressing these problems effectively. However, despite doing all her agreed homework assignments, Carol did not make much progress in therapy. After therapy finished, Carol admitted to her friend that she had several doubts about the treatment plan that she, at least on the surface, was involved in developing with her therapist. She told her friend that she did not tell her therapist her doubts because she did not want to upset her therapist. This was the case even though her therapist had asked her if she had any doubts, reservations or objections to any aspect of therapy.

You Think That Intellectual Insight Is Enough to Help You

In CBT there are two forms of insight, what might be termed "intellectual insight" and "emotional insight." When you have intellectual insight, you understand and agree with some aspect of your therapy, but this insight has not yet impacted on your feelings and behaviour. Emotional insight, on the other hand, does impact on your feelings and behaviour. Thus, you may know that making an important error does not make you a less worthwhile person, but this insight (intellectual) will not impact on your feelings and behaviour until you act on it and keep doing so until you come to believe it. Thus, you may not make much progress in CBT if you believe that intellectual insight is enough to achieve your goals.

You Are Not Prepared to Work for Change

As I have discussed throughout this book, CBT depends on you taking an active role in the therapeutic process both inside and outside the therapy room. So, if you are not prepared to work for change, then you will not make very much progress. Here are some common progress-blocking attitudes that people have in this area:

- "I shouldn't have to help myself, it is my therapist's job to help me."
- "I'm too lazy to help myself."
- "I don't have the time to carry out homework assignments."

If you hold these or similar attitudes, you need to discuss them with your therapist.

You Are Intolerant of the Discomfort and Unfamiliarity Associated With Change

While you can achieve a lot from CBT, you will not do so (i) unless you are prepared for the discomfort of facing up to and discussing painful issues and (ii) unless you are prepared to tolerate the unfamiliarity that you will experience during the process of change. As I often say: "If it isn't strange, it isn't change." So if you are intolerant of such discomfort and feelings of unnaturalness, then you will not make much progress in CBT, and to remedy this, you need to discuss this with your therapist.

Lack of Progress Due to Therapist Factors

So far I have discussed possible reasons why you have not made much progress in CBT that are due to problems in the working alliance that you have with your therapist or to factors within you as a client. However, your therapist may be largely responsible for your lack of progress, and I will briefly discuss some of these therapist factors in this section.

Your Therapist Lacks Important General Therapeutic Skills

One of the most common therapist factors that impedes client progress is that the therapist lacks general therapeutic skills. When a therapist lacks general therapeutic skills:

- She fails to listen to you or empathise with you
- She consistently puts words into your mouth
- She interacts with you in a way that reinforces your problems (e.g. she is too active, and this reinforces your problematic passivity)
- She has unreasonably high or unreasonably low expectations of you, which results in her either pushing you too much or too little
- She is too forceful in making points and fails to elicit or take into account your views
- She misjudges what stage of change you are in and works with you in the wrong stage of change (e.g. she assumes that you are ready to change something when you are, in fact, ambivalent about doing so)

Your Therapist Lacks CBT-Specific Skills

One of the other most common therapist factors that impedes client progress is that the therapist lacks CBT-specific skills. This is why it is important that you check the credentials of your CBT therapist, as there are many therapists who say that they practise CBT when they are not fully qualified to do so. However, consulting a qualified CBT therapist, while important, is no guarantee that the therapist will not lack core CBT-specific skills. When a therapist lacks such skills:

- She fails to understand accurately your problems in CBT terms
- She fails to explain clearly her understanding of your problems even if this may be accurate
- She fails to suggest a CBT approach that, if you both use it properly, will help you deal effectively with your problems
- She suggests an effective CBT approach to your problems but implements this poorly
- She is poor in negotiating and reviewing suitable homework assignments
- She does not identify and address effectively reasons why you may not be making expected progress in CBT

Your Therapist Has Personal Issues/Problems That Interfere With Her Helping You

It is important for you to recognise that your therapist is human and is not immune from the problems and issues that all human beings are capable of experiencing. Having said that, it is realistic for you to expect that whatever problems your therapist may have will not intrude on your therapy. Sadly, this is not always the case, and here are some examples where the therapist's issues/problems do interfere with therapy and may help to explain your lack of progress:

- Your therapist has the same problem as you and has not been able to help herself with that problem, with the result that she fails to offer you credible help

- She believes that she needs your approval, with the result that she fails to confront you appropriately
- She believes that her worth depends on your progress, with the result that she may get angry or defensive if you don't make the progress that she expects
- She has a problem with impatience and seems to get impatient or irritable if you fail to understand something or when therapy does not go smoothly
- She disturbs herself about your problems, with the result that she cannot gain the professional distance she needs to help you effectively

Dealing With Lack of Progress

When you are not making as much progress as you might reasonably expect for one or more of the reasons discussed above (or for other reasons), it is important that you and your therapist address this issue. If you do not do so, it is unlikely that you will be able, on your own, to overcome these obstacles to progress.

Most people would say, rightly in my view, that it is mainly your therapist's responsibility to initiate a discussion concerning these reasons, even if you have brought up the issue of lack of progress in the first place. However, you also have a responsibility to speak up, since your therapist will not be able to read your mind and deal with matters without your active participation in this process. I will discuss both your and your therapist's responsibility for dealing with lack of progress in the rest of this chapter.

Your Therapist's Responsibility for Dealing With Lack of Progress

If your therapist thinks that you are not making progress as expected, then it is important that she brings this to your attention and initiate a discussion about this. Your therapist should preferably also initiate such a discussion when you have brought up the issue of lack of progress. When your therapist initiates such a discussion, then this will go better if she has already established what is known as a "meta-therapy dialogue" with you. This is a technical term which refers to a process where you and your therapist stand back, as it were, and reflect on issues pertaining to therapy. If your therapist has already set up such a dialogue with you, then the subsequent discussion about lack of progress should go more smoothly than if such a dialogue has not yet been established.

Once the discussion about lack of progress has been initiated, there are two major things that your therapist needs to do to increase the chances that this discussion will be fruitful, as discovered by Jeremy Safran and his team at the New School Center for Psychotherapy Research in New York.

Your Therapist Needs to Adopt a Flexible and Negotiable Stance in the Discussion

Safran and his colleagues say that when your therapist does so, then you will say things like:

- "My therapist and I are good at finding a solution if we disagree."
- "I do not feel that I have to pretend to agree with my therapist's goals for our therapy so that the sessions run smoothly."
- "I feel like I have a say regarding what we do in therapy."
- "My therapist is flexible and takes my wants or needs into consideration."
- "I do not feel that my therapist tells me what to do and has regard for my wants or needs."
- "My therapist is flexible in her ideas regarding what we do in therapy."

As you can see from the above statements, when your therapist establishes a flexible and negotiable stance, this will help both of you to reflect on the reasons for your lack of expected progress as a client. Compare this with what you are likely to say if your therapist is rigid and not open to negotiation about possible reasons for your lack of progress.

- "I feel that my therapist tells me what to do, without much regard for my wants or needs."
- "My therapist is inflexible and does not take my wants or needs into consideration."
- "My therapist is rigid in his/her ideas regarding what we do in therapy."
- "I feel like I do not have a say regarding what we do in therapy."
- "I pretend to agree with my therapist's goals for our therapy so the session runs smoothly."
- "My therapist and I are not good at finding a solution if we disagree about what we should be working on in therapy."

Indeed, if your therapist routinely displays such closed mindedness, this may be a prime reason for your lack of progress. Most therapists at times show a closed-minded attitude, but if yours does so routinely, then you may need to consult a different CBT therapist!

Your Therapist Needs to Demonstrate That She Is Comfortable Dealing With Disagreement and With Any Negative Feelings That You Might Express

Safran and his colleagues say that when your therapist does so, then you will say things like:

- "I feel that I can disagree with my therapist without harming our relationship."
- "My therapist encourages me to express any concerns I have with our progress."
- "I am comfortable expressing disappointment in my therapist when it arises."
- "My therapist encourages me to express any anger I feel towards her."
- "My therapist is able to admit when he/she is wrong about something we disagree on."
- "I am comfortable expressing frustration with my therapist when it arises."

As you can see from these statements, if your therapist can comfortably hear and, indeed, invite your negativity about aspects of the therapy and the way in which she is working with you, you are likely to feel able, in turn, to be honest about your negative feelings about your lack of progress and the things that may be hindering such progress. You will also feel free to say what you don't like about the therapy.

Compare this with what you are likely to say if your therapist is uncomfortable dealing with disagreement and with your negative feelings about her or your therapy.

- "I don't feel that I can disagree with my therapist without harming our relationship."
- "My therapist does not encourage me to express any concerns I have with our progress."
- "I am not comfortable expressing disappointment in my therapist when it arises."
- "My therapist does not encourage me to express any anger I feel towards her."
- "My therapist is unable to admit when he/she is wrong about something we disagree on."
- "I am not comfortable expressing frustration with my therapist when it arises."

The chances are that you will be reluctant to be honest about your thoughts and feelings about why you may not be progressing in therapy. Most therapists at times show discomfort about disagreement and about hearing something negative about therapy, but again, if yours does so routinely, a change of CBT therapist may be in order!

Your Therapist Needs to Give You Honest Feedback About How Therapy Is Proceeding and What Factors Might Explain Your Lack of Progress

To the above factors suggested by Safran and his colleagues I would add a third. As well as being able to take bad news as demonstrated above, your therapist also needs to be able to give bad news in offering her opinion about why you may not be making expected progress. A good therapist has the ability to be honest without discouraging you in the process. Thus, if your therapist considers that a major reason for your lack of progress is your failure to apply yourself in a consistent way to carrying out homework assignments, then she should say so, but in a way that shows that you could apply yourself and, as importantly, in a way that engages you in an honest exploration of why you may not be applying yourself as consistently as you might. I should add that it is particularly important for your therapist to be honest if you have unreasonable expectations about change and you are, in fact, making as much progress as you might be expected to be making. Encouraging you to develop more realistic expectations about progress may help you to re-invest in the process of CBT and make advances in a slower, but perhaps more sustained manner.

If your therapist does not give you genuine feedback, she may be depriving you of the opportunity to address some uncomfortable truths which, if addressed, may well help you to make more progress in therapy.

Your Responsibility for Dealing With Lack of Progress

Having outlined what responsibility your therapist has in dealing with your lack of progress, let me be clear and state that you also have responsibility here. My view is that your responsibility is to speak up and be honest. Yes, as we have seen, your therapist can facilitate or hinder you in this regard, but no matter how facilitative your therapist is, you still have a choice whether or not to speak up and be honest. You may well be apprehensive about being assertive in this regard for fear of hurting your therapist's feelings, for example, but if you don't take the risk, particularly when your therapist has demonstrated her flexibility and comfort in dealing with difficult issues, then remember this: your therapist can't help you with something about which she does not know.

However, if you don't feel able to speak up and be honest about something that may be hindering your progress in therapy, then you can talk about your difficulty about doing so. In this, your therapist can help in two ways. First, she can help you overcome your fear of speaking up, and then when you have spoken up, she can help you with whatever you have spoken up about.

Violet was seeking help for a chronic problem with procrastination. She was making good progress with this until her therapist put forward the hypothesis that a component of her problem was due to autonomy issues. She privately disagreed with this hypothesis but told her therapist that she agreed. It was when she stopped making progress that her therapist encouraged a discussion about possible reasons for this. During this discussion, Violet told her therapist that she found it difficult to be honest with him. He helped her to investigate this with him and this then encouraged her to tell him that she thought he was wrong about his autonomy hypothesis. He demonstrated comfort with this feedback, and with therapy properly recalibrated, she began to make progress again.

By identifying and addressing the reasons for your lack of progress, you should be able to make the progress you were expecting and eventually achieve your goals. When this happens, it may be time to end therapy. However, you also have the possibility, if practicable, of learning how to be your own therapist, and I will discuss this issue in the following and final chapter.

Note

1. In this chapter, when I discuss lack of progress, I refer to instances when you are not making as much progress as you might reasonably be expected to be making. You may, of course, have unreasonable expectations of progress with respect to your problems and are, in fact, making expected progress. This is something that your therapist will discuss with you, as I will make clear later in the chapter.

8

Become Your Own CBT Therapist

One of the major goals that your CBT therapist is likely to have is to help you to become your own CBT therapist. This means that you will be helped to develop a number of skills which you will be encouraged to use increasingly for yourself over the course of therapy with the aim of using them for yourself when formal therapy has ended.

While this is a major aim of CBT, it is important to note that as a client you may or may not be interested in learning to use CBT-based self-help skills for yourself after therapy has ended, or if you are, you may be interested in doing this informally in your own way and may not wish to learn these skills in a more structured, formal way. The important point, and one that I have stressed throughout this book, is that effective CBT therapists are prepared to tailor their approaches according to their clients' idiosyncratic situations and preferences. Having said that, in this final chapter, I am going to discuss what you can expect from CBT if you are interested to learn to become your own CBT therapist. In doing so, I will not discuss specific skills that may or may not be relevant to you; rather, I will focus on categories of skills that are likely to have broader relevance.

Learning Assessment Skills

When you are working towards becoming your own CBT therapist, it is important that you learn how to identify the important factors that comprise your reactions to situations that are problematic for you. As part of this process, your therapist may suggest that you use a printed form on which there will be a number of headings and spaces under those headings for you to write down your responses. There are a number of such forms and the one suggested by your therapist may be dictated by the approach to CBT that she practises and/or the nature of your problem(s) for which you are seeking help.

Assessment forms are usually designed to help you to assess specific information. They may or may not include information detailing how to complete them. Once you have filled out such a form on a number of occasions, you will be able to see more general patterns emerge that will help you to anticipate how you may respond so that you can help yourself early on in a problem episode or even in advance of a likely episode. I will discuss this in greater detail later in this final chapter.

Filling in such forms and thus learning to assess your problems involves you being able to do the following:

• Identify the kind of situations you find difficult (e.g. speaking in public)
• Identify what you find particularly disturbing about these situations (e.g. your mind going blank)
• Identify the main troublesome emotions that you experience in these situations and the major physiological expressions of these feelings, if relevant
• Identify the behaviours that you carry out to avoid these situations (or what you find troublesome about them) and the behaviors that you carry out when you are in these situations which may make your problems worse. Here you will also be helped to assess what happens in response to your behaviours
• Identify how you "feel like" acting in these situations but do not convert into overt behaviour
• Identify the most relevant cognitions (e.g. thoughts, beliefs) that you have before, during and after you experience your problem about the troublesome aspects of the situations previously identified

Initially, it is likely that you will be shown how to use the assessment form in a therapy session using a recent problem episode. Here your therapist will take the lead and guide you towards identifying the relevant information by asking you focused questions. She will then probably ask you to complete a new assessment form before the next therapy session on another specific problem episode and will go over your responses at the beginning of that session. She will then give you feedback to help you to use the form more accurately. This process will continue to the point where you can use the form on your own.

After you have become proficient at using the form, you will find that you may be able to carry out an assessment in your head by referring to its categories either before you encounter a troublesome situation or even while you are in the midst of one. If you need help to do this, ask your therapist, if she does not offer such help herself.

Learning Thinking Skills

One of the defining features of most CBT approaches is that thinking, of some sort, is at the heart of troublesome reactions to situations that you find problematic. I have discussed in the previous section that one of the ways in which you can become your own therapist is to learn and apply CBT assessment skills for yourself. One such skill involves you identifying cognitions that underpin your troublesome reactions. Different CBT approaches stress the importance of different types of cognition, and for some of these approaches, the importance of these different types varies across emotional and behavioural problems. This means that if you consult different CBT therapists, you might come away being encouraged to look for different types of cognition as part of learning how to assess your own problems. Here is an example of the different terms that CBT therapists use to categorise problematic thinking:

- Negative automatic thoughts (NATs)
- Thinking distortions
- Maladaptive assumptions
- Dysfunctional attitudes or schemas
- Irrational beliefs

Here is not the place to go into the meaning of such terms. Rather, the point that I wish to make is that the types of cognition that your therapist will help you to focus on will depend, in part, on the problem(s) for which you are seeking help, and, in part, on your therapist's own particular practice of CBT.

A glance at the above terms shows that problematic thinking is categorised as being "negative" in some way and most, but not all, CBT therapists subscribe to this notion. These therapists will go on to help you to respond to such thinking as a means of changing them in some way and will teach you skills to do this for yourself.

However, other CBT therapists contend that such thinking is not negative per se, and makes perfect sense in the context in which you hold these thoughts. What makes such thinking problematic for you, say these CBT therapists, is your relationship with them, categorised largely by your attempts to get rid of them. These therapists will help you to accept the presence of such thinking and show you that you can resume your goal-directed behaviour while accepting its existence. Such practitioners are more likely to teach you what are known as mindfulness-based thinking skills in which, as I have said, you are shown how to accept the presence of "negative" thinking rather than how to modify it. Different CBT therapists will approach the teaching of thinking skills in different ways, and it is important that your CBT therapist finds out from you how you best learn such skills and tailors her interventions accordingly.

Learning "Modifying Thinking Skills"

I mentioned above that in CBT, you can be shown how to modify certain cognitions or to accept their presence. When your therapist teaches you "modifying thinking skills," it is likely that she will do so by using forms that are designed to help you to stand back, ask questions about problematic thinking and formulate healthier (e.g. more useful, more valid, more logical) alternative thinking. As with learning assessment skills, you are first shown how to use the relevant form to modify thinking with reference to an example of one of your problems, then you are encouraged to use the form for this purpose as a homework task and your therapist will offer feedback to refine your thinking modification skills once you have reported on your homework. As you develop competence in these skills, you will find it easier to modify problematic thinking for yourself without using the written forms and you should ideally aim to do this before entering situations in which you experience your problems, while you are in such situations, and after you leave them. Once again, your therapist will help you to use these skills "in your head," should you require such help.

Learning "Acceptance-Based Thinking Skills"

Acceptance-based thinking skills are not generally taught by using written forms; rather they are taught experientially (i.e. by gaining experience in the use of such skills). Here, you may be asked to identify a meaningful metaphor which helps you to digest the idea that you can recognise the existence of something without engaging with it, on the one hand, and without trying to eliminate it, on the other. Your therapist will introduce you to various exercises which will help you to develop these acceptance-based thinking skills and you will be expected to practise these skills in relevant situations. How and at what rate you do this is a matter for negotiation between you and your therapist. Finally, you will be encouraged to practise these skills while pursuing value-based goals.

Learning Behavioural Skills

Another area in which you can learn to be your own CBT therapist involves you acquiring key behavioural skills which will help you to achieve and maintain your goals. Commonly taught behavioural skills in CBT include:

Communication Skills

Here you learn, amongst others, how to:

- listen actively to what others say
- convey your understanding of what they are saying
- and state clearly what you want to say.

These skills are particularly important to developing and maintaining good relationships with others.

Assertion Skills

Here you learn how to state clearly your position on various matters, which serves to help you to maintain healthy boundaries between yourself and others. Assertion skills enable you (i) to convey your negative feelings to others while showing respect for them and, equally important, they also enable you (ii) to convey your positive feelings to them. The skills in the first category are particularly relevant for those who often do what they don't want to do and therefore get taken advantage of in relationships, and the skills in the second category are more relevant for those who other people complain always focus on negative aspects of their relationships to the exclusion of the positive aspects.

Study Skills

Here you learn, amongst others, how to:

- organise what you have to do on a course of study
- digest information
- and convey your ideas in writing to enable you to achieve your academic goals.

These are just a sample of behavioural skills that clients learn in CBT when they do not have such skills in their behavioural repertoire and the acquisition of such skills are important in helping them to achieve and maintain their therapeutic goals.

The Process of Learning Behavioural Skills

While your CBT therapist will help you to learn and internalise the above-mentioned skills in ways that best suit your learning style, acquiring behavioural skills as part of becoming your own CBT therapist is likely to involve some or all of the following steps:

- Your therapist will help you identify the relevant behavioural skill deficit and encourage you to see how learning this skill will help you to achieve your therapeutic goals and how doing so will stand you in good stead for the future. As part of this process, you will be encouraged to share any doubts, reservations or objections to learning the skill which your therapist will discuss with you in full.
- Your therapist will then outline the skill and break it down into its constituent parts and will model this skill for you if necessary and where practicable.
- You will then try out the skill, first in the therapy session if this can be done, and be encouraged to implement the skill in your own personal style.
- Then, you will be encouraged to practise the skill before the next therapy session.
- You will report back on your experiences of implementing the skill and be given feedback on how to refine it.
- Through this process of skill practice and refinement, based on experience and feedback, you will internalise this skill and be able to use it in the future whenever you need to do so.
- During this process of behavioural skill learning and practice, you may encounter a variety of obstacles along the way. I refer you to Chapter 7, where I devoted an entire chapter to identifying and dealing with obstacles to making progress in CBT. I want to make the point here that you should be prepared to disclose such obstacles to skill learning and internalisation to your therapist so that together you may understand and respond effectively to the factors leading to the obstacle.

Learning Emotion Regulation Skills

A recent development in CBT has been the focus that therapists place on helping clients to regulate their distressed emotions so that they don't feel overwhelmed by them. Some of the skills that I have already discussed form a part of you learning to regulate your emotions. Thus, looking for and responding to the thinking that underpins your distressed emotions will generally help to abate them, as will externalizing them in some way, as it is often the act of suppressing these emotions that adds to distress. Thus, communicating respectfully how you feel to another person helps in this regard, as does writing your feelings down. In addition, learning to use mindfulness-based skills, where you acknowledge the presence of your distressed emotion and you continue to pursue your goals without engaging with the emotion or trying to eliminate it, often serves to reduce the subjective nature of your distress.

In addition to these methods, your therapist may use some or all of the following to teach you how to regulate your own distressing emotions:

Developing Unconditional Self-Acceptance

You might find a negative emotion particularly distressing because you are judging yourself negatively for experiencing the emotion. The presence of shame for having a feeling is a good sign that you are doing this (e.g. regarding yourself as childish and less worthwhile for feeling hurt). Here, your therapist may teach you to accept yourself as an ordinary person experiencing an understandable emotion and help you to see that judging yourself on the basis of an experience is neither valid nor helpful to you.

Learning Self-Validation and Self-Compassion

Self-validation occurs when you are able to reassure yourself that what you feel inside is real, is important and makes sense given the circumstances in which you felt it. Self-compassion extends this in three ways, as noted by the psychologist Dr. Kristin Neff: (i) by relating to yourself with kindness, (ii) by encouraging yourself to see that you are not different from others but are a part of common humanity, as we all struggle with distressing feelings at times and (iii) by encouraging the development of a mindful stance for your feelings (as noted above). Your therapist will help you to take these concepts and to use them in everyday ways and suggest the same process of (i) practice, (ii) feedback and (iii) refinement that I discussed earlier in this chapter.

Increasing Distress Tolerance

One of the major reasons why you may find your emotions difficult to regulate is that your stance towards them indicates that you find them intolerable. As a result, you may try to get rid of them or away from them as soon as you begin to experience them or you may attempt to avoid situations in which you predict that you might experience them. Some CBT therapists call this "experiential avoidance," where you literally attempt to avoid experiencing certain emotions. In order to develop a sense of regulation over these emotions, you need to increase your level of tolerance for these emotions. As you do so, you will become less fearful of the emotions and this will help you to deal with the issues that underpin them.

Using Imagery to Deal With Feelings

Approaches to CBT not only focus on thinking that occurs in words; they also focus on thinking that occurs in images. Your therapist can thus help you to use imagery by picturing yourself in troublesome situations and dealing constructively with the feelings that you predict you will experience. Rehearsing such scenarios will help you to become less afraid of your feelings and to face them rather than avoid them.

Using Self-Soothing Skills

In the same way that a mother soothes her baby when the child is upset, you can utilise your five senses to learn to soothe yourself as a means of regulating your distressing emotions.

Learning Relapse Prevention Skills

One very important way in which you can be your own therapist is by learning relapse prevention skills. These involve the following:

- Accepting without liking the reality of lapses or slips (i.e. temporary and non-serious return to your problems)

- Identifying vulnerability factors (i.e. factors both in the environment and inside you that serve as triggers to lapses/slips)
- Developing and rehearsing constructive responses to these vulnerability factors
- Facing up to these vulnerability factors in a sensible way so that you can practise these constructive responses
- Accepting yourself if you relapse (i.e. a more serious and enduring return to your problems) and learning from this experience

Learning to Generalise Your Learning, Becoming Less Prone to Emotional Disturbance in the Future and Pursuing Healthy Self-Development

Whether you have sought help from your CBT therapist for one problem or for several problems, you still have the option to add to your skills as your own therapist once you have achieved what you were seeking from CBT. First, you can generalise your learning; second, you can learn to become less prone to emotional disturbance in the future; and third, you can pursue matters of healthy self-development. Before I discuss these three issues, I want to make clear that addressing them in therapy is dependent on three points: (i) whether or not you want to learn these skills, (ii) whether or not your therapist conceives working with these issues as being a part of her role and (iii) whether or not the context in which you are seeing your therapist permits such work, given the amount of time that needs to be devoted to it.

As with other matters, you need to discuss such issues with your therapist and come to an agreement on them. However, assuming that both of you want to and are able to focus on such issues and, if relevant, you have the support of the organization in which you are being seen, then the following points should be borne in mind.

Learning to Generalise Your Learning

Once you have achieved your therapeutic goal, or one of them if you have several, then you have the option of generalising the learning that you derived from achieving your goal(s) to tackling other problems that you may have. You do this by working with your therapist to identify what you learned, to see if this learning is appropriate to your other problems, and determining a plan based on your learning to tackle these problems, if relevant. Answering the following questions may help you in your discussions with your therapist.

• What recurring thoughts, images and beliefs did I identify as being at the core of my problem(s) and how did I respond constructively to them? Are these thoughts, images and beliefs relevant to my other problems and if so, would responding to them in a similar way also have a constructive impact as I deal with my new problems? If so, how can I best do so?
• What recurring behavioural patterns did I identify as being relevant in understanding how I unwittingly maintained my problems and what more constructive alternative behaviours did I implement in achieving my goals? Are these problematic behaviours also a factor in my other problems and if so, can I also apply the more constructive alternative behaviours that I developed in addressing my previous problems to these new problems?

Becoming Less Prone to Emotional Disturbance in the Future

If you want to become less prone to emotional disturbance in the future, you need to learn and apply general patterns of healthy thinking and constructive behaviour to a range of adversities that are likely to be troublesome for you. Seeking out such adversities, wherever possible and feasible, in a sensible way, while using these general patterns, is probably the best way of doing this. This is best implemented when the task at hand is difficult, but not overwhelming for you. If you and your therapist have decided to work on helping you to become less prone to future emotional disturbance, the extent to which you agree on how you will approach this task is once again important.

Pursuing Healthy Self-Development

Have you ever wondered what is the difference between therapy and coaching? Well, one way of distinguishing the two is that therapy is more concerned with helping you overcome emotional problems, whereas coaching is focused on helping you to pursue goals that are related to healthy self-development. While the differences are, in fact, more blurred than this, in reality, it is a useful rule of thumb when considering the differences between cognitive behaviour therapy (CBT) and cognitive behavioural coaching (CBC) for our purposes. Thus, when you are predominantly working with your therapist on matters largely concerned with promoting your healthy self-development, strictly speaking, you have moved into coaching and this needs to be acknowledged by both of you. Most organisations that offer non-fee-paying therapy do not regard coaching, by this definition, as part of their brief, and if you are paying your therapist a fee and getting reimbursed from a private health organisation, be aware that it is unlikely that they will pay for coaching as opposed to therapy. However, if you are seeing a therapist privately, are not seeking fee reimbursement and your therapist also has coaching as well as therapy skills, then CBC can be seen as a logical extension of successful CBT.

We have now come to the end of this companion guide and I hope you have found it useful and that it has helped you get the most out of your CBT. I would appreciate receiving any feedback that might improve this guide based on your experiences of using it. Please email me on info@windydryden.com

Appendix 1

Therapeutic Contract with Windy Dryden

1. Length of Therapy Sessions

Therapy sessions are 50 minutes in length unless otherwise agreed.

2. Fee

My fee is £................. per session pro rata. The method of payment is by mutual agreement. I will give you two months notice of any increase to my fee.

Please note that as your contract is with me, I expect you to pay me directly. I do not invoice insurance companies, but will provide you with receipts for you to claim reimbursement from them.

3. Cancellation Policy

My cancellation policy is as follows. In order for you to cancel a session without charge you need to give me 48 hours notice. My full fee will be levied if this notice within this period is not given. An exception to this is if you, or a member of your immediate family, suffer a sudden serious illness.

If I cancel a session, I will give you 48 hours notice. If I do not do so, then your next therapy session will be free of charge. An exception to this is if I, or a member of my immediate family, suffer a sudden serious illness.

4. Confidentiality Policy

My confidentiality policy is as follows. All sessions are confidential with the following exceptions:

- If you pose a serious threat to your own life or well-being and are not prepared to take steps to protect yourself, I will take steps to provide such protection.
- If you pose a serious threat to the life or well-being of another person and are not prepared to take steps to protect them, I will take steps to provide such protection.
- If I am legally mandated to make my notes available.
- If my fees are not paid and I take legal recourse to recover these fees.

If you wish me to provide information about our sessions to a third party, I require notification of this request in writing.

5. My Working Environment

- As I do not have waiting room facilities, I would be grateful if you would ring my bell at your appointed appointment time and not before.
- Please do not attend a therapy session if you are intoxicated or are under the influence of a mind-altering drug.
- Also, as the smell of cigarette smoke lingers and may affect other clients whom I may see after your session, I respectfully request that you do not smoke an hour before your session.

I have read, understood and agree to the above points.

Signature of client............... Signature of therapist..................

Print name........................... Print name....................................

Date..................................... Date...

Appendix 2

Possible Reasons for Not Completing Homework (Self-Help) Assignments

The following is a list of reasons that various clients have given for not doing their homework (self-help) assignments during the course of CBT. Because the speed of improvement depends primarily on the amount of such assignments that you are willing to do, it is of great importance to pinpoint any reasons that you may have for not doing this work. It is important to look for these reasons at the time that you feel a reluctance to do your assignment or a desire to put off doing it. Hence, it is best to fill out this questionnaire at that time. If you have any difficulty filling out this form and returning it to your therapist, it might be best to do it together during a therapy session.

Rate each statement by ringing 'T' (True) or 'F' (False). 'T' indicates that you agree with it; 'F' means the statement does not apply at this time.

1. It seems that nothing can help me, so there is
no point in trying.   T/F
2. It wasn't clear, I didn't understand what I had
to do.   T/F
3. I thought that the particular method my therapist
had suggested would not be helpful. I didn't really
see the value of it.   T/F
4. It seemed too hard.   T/F
5. I am willing to do self-help assignments, but
I keep forgetting.   T/F
6. I did not have enough time. I was too busy.   T/F

7. If I do something my therapist suggests I do, it's not as good as if I come up with my own ideas. T/F
8. I don't really believe I can do anything to help myself. T/F
9. I have the impression my therapist is trying to boss me around or control me. T/F
10. I worry about my therapist's disapproval. I believe that what I do just won't be good enough for her. T/F
11. I felt too bad, sad, nervous, upset (underline the appropriate word[s]) to do it. T/F
12. It would have upset me to do the homework. T/F
13. It was too much to do. T/F
14. It's too much like going back to school again. T/F
15. It seemed to be mainly for my therapist's benefit. T/F
16. Homework or self-help assignments have no place in therapy. T/F
17. Because of the progress I've made, these assignments are likely to be of no further benefit to me. T/F
18. Because these assignments have not been helpful in the past, I couldn't see the point of doing this one. T/F
19. I don't agree with this particular approach to therapy. T/F
20. OTHER REASONS (please write them)